Attention Deficit Disorder

Strategies for School-Age Children

Clare B. Jones, Ph.D.

Foreword by
Sam Goldstein, Ph.D.

**Communication
Skill Builders** ®
a division of
The Psychological Corporation

555 Academic Court
San Antonio, Texas 78204-2498
1-800-228-0752

Reproducing Pages from This Book

Many of the pages in this book may be reproduced for instructional or administrative use (not for resale). To protect your book, make a photocopy of each reproducible page. Then use that copy as a master for photocopying.

Dedication

This book is dedicated to the many students
who provided the spark for my work and to

Dr. Arthur W. Hogling, my brother,

and

Dr. Mark Katz, my friend.

Their faith and encouragement kept my lamp burning.

About the Author

Clare Banker Jones received her Ph.D. in education from the University of Akron, her M.A. from Cleveland State University, and her B.S. Ed. from Drake University. A diagnostic specialist, she is certified in teaching children who are learning disabled and mentally retarded. She is a validator for the National Association for the Education for Young Children and was honored by the Martha Holden Jennings Foundation as Master Teacher of the year in 1985. The California Resource Specialists named her Educator of the Year in 1992. She has taught every level of special education from preschool through college. Dr. Jones is former Director of Education at Phoenix Children's Hospital and is currently a faculty associate at Northern Arizona University and Glendale Community College. A nationally known consultant and presenter, Dr. Jones operates a private practice, Developmental Learning Associates, in Phoenix, Arizona. Her first book, *Sourcebook for Children with Attention Deficit Disorder,* was for early childhood professionals and parents.

Contents

List of Figures

Foreword

In 1647 a law was enacted in Massachusetts for the purpose of promoting education among the common people. It was spoken of as the "Old Deluder Law." The real purpose of the law was revealed by the first phrase of the act: the chief object was to prevent Satan, the old deluder, from preventing a man from becoming knowledgeable about the scriptures. By the close of the American Revolutionary War, numerous social, economic, democratic, and national circumstances came into play which made obtaining an education vital for the new American country. Gaining an education helped one obtain material wealth and power. As America grew, industrialization, business methods, scientific achievements, and government increasingly demonstrated that success in these areas demanded schooling. Throughout the nineteenth century, the educational propositions of writers such as Joseph Lancaster and Horace Mann directed that the education of children required pain, fear, and intimidation. Children were perceived as inherently uninterested in the important educational process. But in the twentieth century as America became a melting pot, education became even more vital to help immigrants learn American ways and blend into our society. No longer were children viewed as uninterested in education but rather as hungry for it.

On a daily basis, classroom educators depend upon consistency and predictability in the behavior, attitudes, and educational responses of their students. Managing twenty or thirty children for an hour to six hours per day is not an easy task. If a student is incapable of consistently meeting a classroom task or demand, most teachers are accomplished at making accommodations and adjustments in what is required. When a student performs a similar task well one day but poorly the next, however, teachers are often frustrated and frequently look to faulty characteristics within the student to explain this phenomenon.

Understanding the qualities and behaviors that impair classroom functioning finds a common ground in both logic and science. Children within the classroom either exhibit disruptive, externalizing behaviors which annoy teachers and their classmates or exhibit a set of nondisruptive, internalizing symptoms that frequently invoke worry from teachers. The former consist of problems typically thought to relate to noncompliance, the latter to emotional distress and developmental delay. At the mild end of the disruptive realm, however, are a set of qualities that do not result from purposeful noncompliance but rather from a child's incompetent, inconsistent ability to apply skills he or she may well possess. This pattern of difficulty—characterized by an inability to attend consistently to repetitive, uninteresting activities requiring effort and not of the child's choosing; an inability to allow sufficient time to think before acting and to benefit from experience; a tendency to overreact physically and emotionally to events in the classroom; and difficulty responding to both positive and negative consequences in a way similar to other children—has been identified by the educational, medical, and mental health community as Attention Deficit Hyperactivity Disorder (ADHD). Within a classroom setting, these characteristics create handicaps in a child's ability to complete work, remain seated, and not disrupt the classroom. The two most important student qualities in a classroom are the capabilities to sustain attention and complete work. It is with exactly these two areas that children with Attention Deficit Hyperactivity Disorder struggle.

While the debate concerning the diagnosis and cause of ADHD rages on, within a classroom setting we do not treat the cause nor do we treat the diagnosis. We treat the specific behaviors that impair a student's ability to function effectively and be a successful member of the classroom. In her first text, *Sourcebook for Children with Attention Deficit Disorder: A Management Guide for Early Childhood Professionals and Parents*, Clare Jones offered an exquisitely simple yet eminently practical model based on three simple tenets: Brevity, Variety, and Structure. This model best exemplifies the types of environmental changes, classroom activities, and strategies educators can use to successfully manage and educate students with ADHD. This model fits the research data suggesting that helping students with ADHD become more invested in the task or more interested in the payoff for completing a task can and does dramatically improve their classroom behavior, interest, and work completion.

In this new volume, *Attention Deficit Disorder: Strategies for School-Age Children*, Clare Jones extends her model beyond the preschool years and offers her practical educational and clinical knowledge to assist educators in working with these children in the classroom. This volume moves beyond those texts that focus excessively on managing the behavior of children with ADHD to the more relevant issue of helping them become educated. The volume focuses not on what teachers must stop doing, but rather on what they must do. Clare's sensitivity and respect for children is blended with a set of proven and practical strategies. An added bonus in this text is a section dealing with adult ADHD.

The American educational system has responded to the challenge to educate all children, including those with process-related problems such as ADHD. This text takes that mandate into the twenty-first century. It will make a significant contribution in the educational lives of children with ADHD and their teachers.

Sam Goldstein, Ph.D.
Neurology, Learning and Behavior Center
Clinical Instructor, University of Utah School of Medicine

Chapter 1
Attention Deficit Disorder

Last night, I asked him, "Please clean your room." Twenty minutes later, I went into his room to check up on him and found him playing with his *Legos*® on the floor.
—Father of a 7-year-old boy

He's a wonderful kid . . . delightful! And I just know he can do it. One day, he can hand in an A paper, but the next day, an F. He just doesn't seem to pay attention.
—Teacher of a fifth grader

What's most frustrating about my daughter is when we spend four hours working on homework, she complains the entire time. We finally fall into bed exhausted from arguing, and the next day, she forgets to hand in the paper.
—Parent of an 11-year-old girl

He constantly has something in his hand. I take away the micro-machine, and he has a paper clip. Remove that, and he has an eraser top. Take that away, and he has a broken pencil; it's never-ending!
—Teacher of a second grader

Carol is such a sweet child, but most of the time in my class, she is in "la-la land."
—Teacher of a third grader

For children with attention deficit disorder and their teachers and parents, these comments are part of daily life. Comments regarding inattention, impulsivity, and hyperactivity decorate their report cards, highlight parent-teacher conferences, and in general, describe much of their lives.

Attention Deficit Disorder (ADD/ADHD) is a disorder that involves a short attention span, impulsivity, and difficulty focusing or concentrating. This disorder typically causes the individual to have difficulties feeling satisfied, to be highly active, and to be socially immature. Children with ADD/ADHD experience memory difficulties and perform inconsistently.

Each child with an attention disorder is unique, but these children have common characteristics or anomalies that clearly identify them as having the disorder. They are affected by the disorder to different degrees, but the majority fall within the defining descriptors in the *Diagnostic Statistical Manual of Mental Disorders* (DSM IV; American Psychiatric Association 1994). This manual, the standard reference for classifying psychological conditions, lists 15 symptomatic behaviors, of which 8 must be present in order to make a diagnosis of an attention deficit. The behaviors are as follows (American Psychiatric Association, in press; reproduced with permission):

DSM IV Draft Criteria for Attention-Deficit/Hyperactivity Disorder

A. Either (1) or (2):

    (1) Inattention: At least six of the following symptoms of inattention have persisted for at least six months to a degree that is maladaptive and inconsistent with developmental level:

        (a) often fails to give close attention to details or makes careless mistakes in schoolwork, work, or other activities

        (b) often has difficulty sustaining attention in tasks or play activities

        (c) often does not seem to listen to what is being said to him or her

        (d) often does not follow through on instructions and fails to finish schoolwork, chores, or duties in the workplace (not due to oppositional behavior or failure to understand instructions)

        (e) often has difficulties organizing tasks and activities

        (f) often avoids or strongly dislikes tasks (such as schoolwork or homework) that require sustained mental effort

        (g) often loses things necessary for tasks or activities (e.g., school assignments, pencils, books, tools, or toys)

        (h) is often easily distracted by extraneous stimuli

        (i) often forgetful in daily activities

    (2) Hyperactivity-Impulsivity: At least four of the following symptoms of hyperactivity-impulsivity have persisted for at least six months to a degree that is maladaptive and inconsistent with developmental level:

    Hyperactivity

        (a) often fidgets with hands or feet or squirms in seat

        (b) leaves seat in classroom or in other situations in which remaining seated is expected

        (c) often runs about or climbs excessively in situations where it is inappropriate (in adolescents or adults, may be limited to subjective feelings of restlessness)

        (d) often has difficulty playing or engaging in leisure activities quietly

    Impulsivity

        (e) often blurts out answers to questions before the questions have been completed

        (f) often has difficulty waiting in lines or awaiting turn in games or group situations

B. Onset no later than seven years of age.

C. Symptoms must be present in two or more situations (e.g., at school, work, and at home).

D. The disturbance causes clinically significant distress or impairment in social, academic, or occupational functioning.

E. Does not occur exclusively during the course of a Pervasive Developmental Disorder, Schizophrenia or other Psychotic Disorder, and is not better accounted for by a Mood Disorder, Anxiety Disorder, Dissociative Disorder, or a Personality Disorder.

Code based on type:

314.00 Attention-deficit/Hyperactivity Disorder, Predominantly Inattentive Type: if criterion A(1) is met but not criterion A(2) for the past six months

314.01 Attention-deficit/Hyperactivity Disorder, Predominantly Hyperactivity-Impulsive Type: if criterion A(2) is met but not criterion A(1) for the past six months.

314.02 Attention-deficit/Hyperactivity Disorder Combined Type: if both criteria A(1) and A(2) are met for the past six months.

Coding note: for individuals (especially adolescents and adults) who currently have symptoms that no longer meet full criteria, "in partial remission" should be specified.

The three essential features of the disorder as described in the DSM IV are "developmentally inappropriate degrees of attention, impulsivity, and hyperactivity." These three symptoms can affect how the person functions at home, at school, in the workplace, and in social situations. Although there seems to be a heterogenous group of children with wide variations in difficulty with attention, impulsivity, and hyperactivity, two subgroups also emerge: children who have attention deficit disorder with hyperactivity (ADHD), and those who have attention deficits, inattentive type, without hyperactivity (ADD). Both conditions can be mild, moderate, or severe (see Figure 1). Although the latest edition of the DSM distinguishes between ADD and ADHD, the strategies described in this book are generally applicable to children with a variety of attention concerns. Unless the text specifies attention deficit with hyperactivity or without hyperactivity, the reader can assume that the information is generic to both types of attention deficits.

Figure 1
Criteria for Grading Severity of
Attention Deficit Hyperactivity Disorder

Mild: Few if any symptoms in excess of those required to make the diagnosis and no or only minimal impairment in school and/or social functioning.

Moderate: Symptoms of functional impairment intermediate between "mild" and "severe."

Severe: Many symptoms in excess of those required to make the diagnosis, plus significant and pervasive impairment in functioning at home, in school, and with peers.

3

Of the 15 characteristics in the DSM IV definition, criterion (2)(a) ("Often fidgets with hands or feet or squirms in seat"), is the behavior most frequently reported in national field trials of the descriptive criteria (American Psychiatric Association, in press). The high level of activity usually present during early childhood appears to peak around age five or six, and then begins a slow downward trend. By adolescence, overactivity is generally less apparent and appears more as restlessness.

Children who do not experience the hyperactivity component of the diagnosis tend to be overly passive, lethargic, and somewhat anxious. They tend to have a flat affective style. One teacher described this type of student as "slug-like." Children who have attention deficit disorder without hyperactivity (ADD) generally are quiet and have a timid, rather unassuming social style. They frequently go unnoticed in school, as they generally are quiet and withdrawn rather than being behavior problems. They are often described as "unmotivated."

Possible Causes of Attention Deficit Disorder

Research regarding the causes of ADD/ADHD remains inconclusive, but there is strong evidence linking the condition to genetic, prenatal, environmental, or physical factors. Studies of children with attention deficit reveal that they generally have noticeable behavior differences from birth (Wender 1987).

Current clinical research supports the hypothesis that altered brain biochemistry is a factor in ADD/ADHD. In 1985, Carolyn Hartsough and Nadine Lambert found a strong relationship between attention deficit and prenatal and perinatal problems. They found several significant factors. On average, the mothers of hyperactive children were more likely to report poor health during pregnancy and to be under the age of 20 when the child was born. During their pregnancies, mothers of hyperactive children frequently reported *toxemia* (an infection that results in bacterial toxins circulating in the bloodstream) or *eclampsia* (coma or convulsions associated with high blood pressure). In addition, hyperactive children were twice as likely as normals to have evidence of fetal distress, head injuries, or other birth insults. They also more frequently had medical problems or some type of physical malformation at birth.

Additional compelling research points to hereditary factors as a cause of the disorder. Attention deficit is believed to be more common in first-degree biological relatives. Strong genetic factors have been traced in families (Goldstein and Goldstein 1990; Comings 1990; Wender 1987). Quite frequently, when I am speaking with a family regarding the diagnosis of an attention deficit, the father might state, "I had similar problems when I was a child. But they didn't seem as severe as the ones my daughter has." Or the mother might relate, "My brother has had many of these difficulties, and I just don't want my son to grow up like my brother."

It is now recognized that such genetic traits as eye color and hair color are related to neurotransmitters, and that temperamental differences can also result from the production of particular chemicals in the body. Dr. Bernard Shaywitz (1987, 197) states:

> Evidence from several lines of investigation now supports the belief that such genetic biological factors may be related to abnormalities in neurological function, in particular to disturbance in brain neurochemistry involving a class of brain neurochemicals termed "neurotransmitters"—specifically those neurotransmitters known as catecholamines.

Lead poisoning has been suggested as a possible cause of attention deficit disorder. Lead poisoning can result in neurological damage and certainly destroys neurotransmitters. Wyngaarden (1988) has done extensive research in this area.

Approximately one-third of children with confirmed lead poisoning have some symptoms of attention deficit disorder.

Research into the area of dietary effects—particularly the influences of food additives and simple sugars—is ongoing (Conners 1980). Researchers are looking for possible causal relationships between diet and children's behavior. Although provocative, none of this research has produced dramatic evidence, however, and further investigation is required.

One of the strongest pieces of research currently available regarding the etiology of attention deficit disorder was done by Allen Zametkin and his research team at the National Institute of Mental Health (1990). Using the PET SCAN (Positron Emission Tomography) machine, they were able to show that the rate at which the brain uses glucose—its main energy source—was lower in subjects with hyperactivity of childhood onset as compared with normals. They reported these landmark findings in the *New England Journal of Medicine* in November 1990, and their research is continuing today.

In the PET SCAN procedure, radioactive substances that emit positrons are used to label glucose, which is then introduced into the body by injection so that it may be traced in the brain. Using the PET SCAN, the glucose can be tracked as it is absorbed by the brain and used as fuel. The most active parts of the brain use the largest amounts of glucose.

Zametkin and his researchers have determined that the frontal lobes of the brain are involved in regulating attention, emotional responses, and activity level. In addition, the frontal lobes play a role in planning, an area in which children with attention disorders typically have great difficulty. Children or young adults who have had some type of damage in the frontal lobe area seem to have great difficulty controlling impulsive actions. Although they are able to function in a perfectly normal intelligence range, their ability to plan and to abide by rules seems to be impaired. Hence, Zametkin's research conclusively demonstrates that neurotransmitters play a role in behavior, concentration, and impulsivity. This ongoing PET SCAN research is certainly extremely important in beginning to understand the causes of an attention disorder.

In the April 1993 issue of the *New England Journal of Medicine*, Dr. Peter Hauser at the National Institute of Diabetes, Digestive, and Kidney Diseases in Bethesda, Maryland, reported that ADHD can result from a mistake in a gene that regulates the body's use of the thyroid hormone. Although this gene anomaly probably accounts for only a fraction of the cases of hyperactivity, other thyroid-hormone problems may turn out to be a factor in many cases. Hauser concluded that thyroid hormone pills may help relieve the symptoms of hyperactivity, especially in cases where stimulants have failed.

Prevalence

Attention deficit is one of the more frequent childhood disorders, and it is the single most common reason why children are referred to child mental health clinics today (Barkley 1981). The high prevalence of attention deficit disorder suggests that no teacher will ever teach again without having a child with attention deficit in the classroom. The most commonly cited figures conservatively estimate that attention deficits occur in between 1 and 6 percent of children (Lambert, Sandoval, and Sassone 1978). Shaywitz and Shaywitz (1991) suggest that attention deficits affect 10 to 20 percent of the school-age population. In a survey of more than 2,000 third and fourth graders in Arizona, Hepworth, Jones, and Sehested (1991) found a prevalence of 14 percent. With a disorder that has the range of causes which this one appears to have, we are bound to see a population of significant size.

For more than half of the people diagnosed with attention deficit disorder, the DSM definition places the onset of the disorder no later than age 7, and symptoms may persist into adulthood. The condition continues to be reported more commonly in boys (by about 5 to 1) and is often recognized later in life for girls. Boys tend to be diagnosed before the age of 8, while girls tend to be diagnosed around the age of 12. It is a consistent finding that girls are more frequently diagnosed with ADD than with ADHD.

Treatment: What Works?

Research indicates that the most effective form of management is a multimodality intervention that includes parent training; individual, group, and family psychotherapy; medical management; and interventions aimed at improving school performance (see Figure 2).

At the January 1993 National Forum on the Education of Children with ADD held in Washington, D.C., representatives from four national centers where different aspects of attention deficits are studied gave presentations. (The four centers are among several projects funded by the Department of Education, Office of Special Education Programs.) The overall recommendation on serving the child with an attention disorder was to create a flexible program that involves children and families through school interventions. Strong evidence was provided to support behavior therapy as a successful intervention when it is carried out properly and effectively. Tom Fiore of the Research Triangle Park center reported that providing simple positive reinforcements and mixing group with individual rewards seemed to be the most promising behavior management technique. Other recommended treatments included medication, educational intervention, and parent education. The conclusion was that these interventions could be recommended with guarded optimism.

Figure 2
What Works?

If we respect that each child is unique, then the treatment plan for each child should be unique. The following strategies are frequently effective with the child who has ADD/ADHD. They are *not* listed in any specific order.

Family Understanding of Attention Disorder: parent training, counseling, and support

Behavior Therapy: consistent behavior intervention based on positive reinforcement and mixing group and individual rewards; the use of *response cost*—that is, losing tokens for undesirable behavior

A Healthy Sense of Self-Esteem: experiences of success in which peer and family response to the child is positive and immediate

Medical Interventions: drug therapy as a short-term treatment

Educational Interventions: appropriate educational accommodations provided by knowledgeable teachers

Counseling: training in social skills, coping skills, and goal-directed strategies

6

Commonly Prescribed Medications

Research suggests that at least three classes of behavior-modifying drugs are useful in the management of an attention disorder:

1. Stimulants
2. Antidepressants
3. Antihypertensive Clonidine

Stimulants. Stimulant drug therapy remains a controversial treatment for children with attention deficit disorder. As a short-term tactic, however, it is perceived as highly effective. Surveys suggest that between 1 and 2.6 percent of the school-age population is currently being treated with stimulants for attention deficit symptoms.

The most commonly prescribed stimulants are *Ritalin* (methylphenidate hydro-chloride), *Dexedrine* (D-amphetamine) and *Cylert* (pemoline). These three stimulants are termed "rapid acting" because they produce effects within 45 minutes after ingestion, and the effects peak within 3 to 4 hours. Because of their fast-acting, fast-exiting effects, they are often prescribed two or three times daily.

When a child takes a psychostimulant, the result often is increased attention, reduced impulsivity, and decreased task-irrelevant activities. As a result, teachers observe that the student appears more focused in the classroom. For example, students who typically had been forgetting the multiplication tables begin routinely remembering them. Homework assignments are more frequently turned in on time, and papers are completed during assigned class periods. The reason for these changes is that, with medication, the student is able to concentrate longer, complete activities, and return papers by their deadlines.

In 1993, James Swanson, Project Director of the Child Development Center at the University of California, Irvine, shared research showing that some 60 to 90 percent of children diagnosed with ADHD received stimulant therapy for prolonged periods during their schooling. According to Swanson, over the short-term teachers can expect from students receiving pharmacological treatment more self-control, better concentration, less hostility, fewer behavior problems, more cooperation, and more academic productivity. Swanson cautions, however, that educators cannot expect large changes in academic skills or higher-order processes. Stimulant medications apparently do not boost academic achievement or relieve antisocial behavior or depression. In his study, Swanson equated the expectation that medication will cure attention deficit to giving a child glasses to improve vision, then expecting the child to spontaneously begin reading. "You still have to teach them to read," Swanson says.

Side effects do occur with stimulants. The major side effect is mild insomnia, which occurs in about 70 percent of cases (Conners 1989). Another side effect is appetite reduction. The child will typically pick at lunch and not appear hungry. For some children, this may result in temporary growth suppression, but the effect appears to be quite minor. Sometimes adjusting the child's mealtimes or providing an after-school snack may eliminate this difficulty.

In the 1 to 2 percent of children with ADHD who exhibit a tic disorder—such as a gesture, twitch, or uncontrolled laugh—the condition may be exacerbated by medication. Sometimes the physician will experiment with a lower dosage to see if the condition abates; if not, the medication may have to be eliminated.

Antidepressants. The use of tricyclic antidepressants—including imipramine, desipramine, and bupropion—has also recently been proposed in the literature. The use of a tricyclic antidepressant is helpful, particularly in cases where children have had difficulty taking stimulants. Long-term treatment effects have not been as successful as those of stimulants; therefore, antidepressants are generally prescribed in limited amounts and most frequently only for those children who have significant mood disturbances.

The effects of stimulants have been well documented over many years. Less is known, however, about the effects of antidepressants. These are typically taken twice a day, and their effect is longer-lasting than that of stimulants. They tend to increase attending behavior, increase verbal/gestural communication, and decrease some of the disruptive behavior symptoms. Elevation in mood may also occur for those children who have had difficulty with depression and anxiety. There are some side effects, such as drowsiness and dry mouth. Some children have been reported to develop a skin rash, and others have developed sluggish reactions and focusing in the optic lens that mimics nearsightedness.

Antihypertensives. The last group of drugs that has been used successfully in the management of ADD/ADHD is antihypertensive drugs—specifically clonidine. Clonidine acts on the brain center that controls adrenergic functions (locus coeruleus). It has been used frequently in the past to treat high blood pressure in adults, but some research has pointed to positive effects on behavior. In some cases, clonidine has reduced hyperactivity and impulsivity. Overall results have not been as positive as with stimulants, though. Side effects of clonidine include dry mouth, drowsiness, fatigue, headache, dizziness or sedation, and sometimes psychosis. There have been reported reactions of delirium and hallucinations.

Educators are never in a situation where they are able to prescribe or even recommend the use of medication. Doing so requires the expertise of a psychiatrist or a physician. But as informed consumers and knowledgeable professionals, educators do need to be aware of the medications that the students in their care may be taking. Figure 3 summarizes the variety of drug classes typically used today with children in schools. It identifies the class, common name, technical name, and some possible positive and negative side effects that educators may observe in school.

Figure 3
Commonly Prescribed Medications for ADD/ADHD

Drug Class	Common Name	Technical Name	Possible In-School Effects

Stimulants	Ritalin
	Dexedrine
	Cylert[1]
		Methylphenidate
		    hydrochloride
		Dextroamphetamine
		Pemoline
			+ Increases attention
			+ Controls impulsiveness
			+ Reduces task-irrelevant
			    activity
			+ May increase compliance
			+ May improve writing
			– May reduce appetite
			– May restrict range of
			    emotional responses
			– May result in mild insomnia
			– May cause tics to occur
			[1] – Licking of lips, finger picking

Tricyclic
Antidepressants
	Tofranil
	Norpramin
	Wellbutrin
	Elavil
		Imipramine
		Desipramine
		    hydrochloride
		Bupropion
		Amitriptyline
			+ Increases attending behavior
			+ Increases verbal/gestural
			    communication
			+ Decreases depression/anxiety
			+ Decreases disruptive behavior
			– Some effects on cardiovascular
			    system
			– Dry mouth, constipation

Antihypertensives	Catapres	Clonidine
		    hydrochloride
			+ Reduces hyperactivity
			+ Reduces impulsivity
			+ Decreases aggressive behavior
			– Less effective than stimulants
			    in increasing attention
			– May trigger delirium,
			    hallucinations

For further information refer to: Yudofsky, Stuart C., Robert E. Hales, and Tom Ferguson. 1991. *What you need to know about psychiatric drugs*. New York: Ballantine Books.

Any treatment program using medication must be monitored diligently through periodic follow-up visits to a physician and distribution of observation checklists for recognizing side effects to all adults who have significant contact with the child. Parents need to be made aware of the purpose of the medication, its possible side effects, and the reason why it is being considered. Only then can they make an informed decision about its use.

Understanding the Limitations of Medications

The use of a stimulant medication alone is not the "magic answer" for treating attention deficit—there are no quick and easy answers. Treatment must involve multimodality intervention, and when it does, the improvement is definite and ongoing. If we respect that each child is unique, then the treatment must also be unique to that child. Children's individual treatment plans are determined by their physical status, their genetic background, the severity of their symptoms, and other considerations.

There are a variety of books available to help children understand why they are taking medication. To assist a child in understanding this situation, teachers or parents might select a book featuring a child experiencing similar challenges. Bibliotherapy can be a very effective building block upon which to found the child's comprehension of the medication. The books listed in Figure 4 are recommended to help children understand the role of medication in their lives. They would be appropriate for a school librarian to order.

Figure 4
Resources for Helping Children
Understand Attention Deficit

These books and videos will aid a child's understanding, not only of the attention disorder, but also of the use of medication.

- *Eagle Eyes: A Child's View of Attention Deficit Disorder,* by Jeanne Gehret, M.A.

- *I'm Somebody Too,* by Jeanne Gehret, M.A.

- *I Would if I Could: A Teenager's Guide to ADHD Hyperactivity,* by Michael Gordon, Ph.D.

- *Jumping Johnny, Get Back to Work,* by Michael Gordon, Ph.D.

- *Making the Grade: An Adolescent Struggles with ADD,* by Roberta N. Parker.

- *My Brother Is a World-Class Pain: A Sibling's Guide to ADHD,* by Michael Gordon, Ph.D.

- *Putting on the Brakes,* by Patricia O. Quinn, M.D., and Judith Stern, M.A.

- Also available for children is a video, *It's Just Attention Disorder: A Video for Kids,* by Sam Goldstein, Ph.D., and Michael Goldstein, M.D.

Both parents and children need to be aware of some of the common myths that are associated with medication. Children who respond successfully to the medication also need to have their self-esteem reinforced, so that they feel they can contribute to their success. Several times, I have been in a classroom to hear a teacher berate a child with, "John, you must not be on your medication. You're uncontrollable today. Did you go to the nurse today to get your medication?" This is a negative message. It certainly conveys to the child that he or she is incapable of behaving as required without medication. I have also heard some children tell nurses, "Quick, give me my 'good pill,' I've been bad." I hope the bibliotherapy and video suggested in Figure 4 will help children and professionals to understand the role medication plays. Parents understanding the medication and professionals refraining from negative comments about the child's behavior will all help support this child in the school setting.

In my office one day, a couple related a wonderful anecdote. Their 6-year-old son, who had been on medication for about a year, was told by his family physician, "Gee, Alex, you're doing so much better on the medication. It really makes you behave."

"No, doctor," replied Alex, "I'm the one that gets my medication to work. If it wasn't for me working with it, it wouldn't make any difference at all."

This attitude, reinforced by his parents, has enabled Alex to feel more in control of his life and his attention disorder.

Counseling as Part of the Treatment

Counseling and individual therapy are often appropriate in a multimodality approach when children need help understanding their behaviors and how to manage them. For some children, however, the one-to-one situation during counseling is not productive. The child may appear verbal and dynamic in the session, and the counselor finds him or her enjoyable. But there is very little therapeutic carryover from the session. Children with ADD/ADHD tend to be more successful in peer group situations or social skills training groups, where they have the opportunity to interact with others and actually witness the benefit of the skills they are learning through their peers' reactions.

Behavior Modification

Behavior modification seems to be most effective when it is used in combination with medication. It is a means of managing the child's behavior problems, and the effects do not seem to last if the program is stopped. Implementing a behavior modification program requires an understanding of behavior modification and great effort on the professional's part. Often the school psychologist or local mental health practitioner can assist in designing a behavior modification program. Behavior modification is based on the premise that specific behaviors are learned because they produce specific effects. When negative consequences are attached to a behavior—such as a delay in or removal of a positive event—this should produce some reduction in the behavior.

In general, the use of *response cost* seems to be very successful for children with an attention deficit. In this strategy, teachers reinforce positive behavior by rewarding the students with tokens or points. These points are later redeemed for particular rewards—such as reduced homework, a hall pass, early dismissal, free time, or use of a tape recorder. The students can also lose their tokens for specific undesirable behaviors. An example of the use of a response cost system is given in Chapter 3.

Behavior modification programs can be very positive, but their success depends on the professional's training and the specific setting in which the behavior is expected to occur. One teacher related to me that a behavior-reward program never worked in her classroom. She described her program as follows: if a child was good for a week, on Friday the child would be able to have a popcorn party. Needless to say, the child never achieved the expected five consecutive days of good behavior, and the reward was never given. As a result, the teacher felt that behavior modification programs were ineffective. Had she understood more about behavioral programs and how they are designed, she would have realized that first, the reward must be more immediate, and second, her target behavior, "being good," was too general to be effective.

Educational Interventions

Educational interventions are a significant part of a multimodality treatment. Children with attention deficit generally spend the majority of their time mainstreamed in a regular classroom, and it is in this setting that they must demonstrate the bulk of their academic and social interaction skills. It is important, therefore, that the classroom teacher understand the strengths and weaknesses of these children and be able to implement sound educational strategies within that environment.

It is helpful for teachers to understand attention deficit disorder and know what to expect. They will certainly be more successful if they have benefitted from inservice training in how to teach and manage students with ADD/ADHD in the classroom. Talking with the child's parents and learning what strategies have worked at home is extremely important. Often the parents have sought help from professionals in the community and have learned a variety of techniques that they can share with the teacher. Through learning about each child's needs, teachers can assist with behavioral control, which in turn will help both the child and the teacher feel more successful.

Just as the intervention plan for a child with attention deficits is a multimodality program, so is the educational plan. School personnel will be more successful when they collaborate with one another and share input on managing this child. Guidance counselors, school psychologists, diagnostic resource specialists, social workers, and school nurses can be excellent resources. Children with attention deficit will be more successful when they are served by a team approach.

What Doesn't Work?

Because such a large population is affected by this disorder, there is always a danger that undocumented and poorly researched techniques will begin to glut the market as people search for a "quick fix." Therefore, it is helpful when nationally recognized support groups—such as CHADD, the Association for Children with Learning Disabilities, and the Council for Exceptional Children—provide expert advice about the most appropriate techniques currently available. As family members and professionals working with children with ADD/ADHD, we need to inform ourselves about what treatments have proven effective—and what treatments have *not*.

Research has clearly documented that the following controversial treatments for attention deficit disorder *are not justified as treatments*. This information has been obtained from a variety of resources, including Dr. Sam Goldstein's and Dr. Barbara Ingersoll's report, "Controversial Treatments for Children with Attention Deficit Disorder" in the Fall/Winter 1992 issue of *CHADDER*, and the paper "Legal and Psychological Issues Concerning Attention Deficit-Hyperactivity Disorder," presented in May 1991 by Dr. Wayne Jones and Patrick W. McGee at The Twelfth National Institute on Legal Issues of Educating Individuals with Disabilities.

Dietary interventions. There is no research showing that reducing food coloring, food additives, and sugar in a child's diet offers significant help to children with learning and attentional problems.

Megavitamin therapy. The American Psychiatric Association and the American Academy of Pediatrics have concluded that there is no information justifying the use of very high doses of vitamins and minerals to treat behavioral or learning problems.

Optometric vision training. Optometric vision training is practiced by an optometrist who specializes in an area called behavioral optometry. It is based on the proposition that reading disorders and attentional problems are caused by visual problems such as faulty eye movements. The American Academy of Pediatrics, The American Academy of Ophthalmology and Otolaryngology, and the American Association of Ophthalmology state that there is no evidence that these programs are effective in treating reading or attention disorders.

Chiropractory treatment. The science of applied kinesiology suggests that learning disabilities and attentional problems are caused by the misalignment of two specific bones in the skull. No research has been done to support the effectiveness of this form of treatment, and Ingersoll and Goldstein (1993, 202) state, "This approach to treating learning disabilities is far outside the mainstream of current thought and clinical process. It has no place in the treatment of learning disabled children."

Biofeedback: an inconclusive treatment. The newest entrant into the realm of controversial treatments for attention deficit disorder is biofeedback technology. Biofeedback technology contends that by using an EEG (electroencephalogram), children can be trained to alter their brain waves to improve their concentration and behavior. Dr. Joel Lubar at the University of Tennessee has researched and worked with biofeedback for the last sixteen years. He has developed a rationale for the diagnosis and treatment of attention deficit disorder employing EEG biofeedback techniques. The program involves between 40 and 80 sessions and is integrated with academic work. Children are gradually phased out of the program and followed for a long period of time. Dr. Lubar feels that properly conducted biofeedback training, although time-consuming, can lead to very significant changes in EEG measures, as well as to improvements in psychometric test measures and school performance. He believes he has worked with enough children to have confidence that the EEG biofeedback works very well.

In response to Dr. Lubar, Dr. Russell Barkley contends that the information and research was not collected in a scientifically valid way. He believes that this treatment still needs complete and thorough investigation and advises parents to proceed with caution. The average biofeedback session is costly—somewhere between $2,000 and $5,000—and a long period of time is required for the student to master the technique. To date, no research has been done to determine its long-term effect. Research is ongoing, but the results have not been strong enough to substantiate the claims made by its proponents. Parents of children who have tried the therapy have given it mixed reviews. Biofeedback will continue to be an area of exploration and interest.

Multidisciplinary Diagnosis

The child with suspected attention deficits benefits from evaluation by a multidisciplinary team. This team approach in managing attention deficits brings together individuals from different disciplines who contribute their expertise, share in decision making, and provide strategies for intervention. The multidisciplinary team process is not new, and for a child with documented special needs, it is a requirement under federal law (PL 94-142). The value of a team or collaborative approach for the child with an attention disorder is that it offers a well-defined reservoir of data on the child and provides complementary interpretations from a variety of professionals.

Team members serving children should be trained in all aspects of child development. The needs of each child influence the membership of the team. As a particular pattern of strengths or weaknesses emerges during diagnostic testing, professionals from other disciplines may be invited to join the team, in order to better meet the child's needs. The collaborative team approach is possible in medical settings, in educational environments, and in mental health or other facilities. Parents should be integral members of the team in any setting.

The referral system within the school typically follows this format.

1. Parents voice their concerns to the classroom teacher or the classroom teacher identifies a child as having unique needs and shares these concerns with the parents.

2. The child is referred to a child study team, where professionals at that grade level discuss, suggest, and recommend remediation techniques to the regular classroom teacher. Some schools call the child study team a "teacher assistance" team (TAT), but the purpose of the team remains to address the needs and difficulties of the child and determine how best to meet those needs. The team should ensure that the child's problems are clearly stated. The team reviews the child's background and educational records, any updated educational information, and all other pertinent information. Then the teacher returns to the classroom with the child study team's recommendations and, in collaboration with the parents, begins to try the team's suggestions.

3. Referral for special education evaluation occurs only after other alternatives have been tried and have proven unsuccessful within the regular classroom. The teacher needs to evaluate whether appropriate instructional alternatives have been provided in the regular classroom and whether the student's needs can be met only with further services. If the child study team then determines that further educational evaluation of the child is necessary, this procedure will begin to take place in the school. Parental permission to evaluate must be obtained, and procedural safeguards must be followed.

Assessment

No one norm-referenced psychometric assessment battery has been developed for all children with attention deficit. Clinical evaluation must include a quantitative assessment by the examiner of the child's attention, problem solving, and reflection skills. It should also include a self-report questionnaire or task checklist in addition to a clinical interview with the parents and a physical history of the child. Observation, usually by the classroom teacher, is the initial tool in documenting the child's level of attention and distractibility. Observation should occur in a variety of settings and should address the following issues:

1. How does the child work independently?

2. How does the child interact with peers?

3. How does the child perform in different environments, such as in gym class, during assembly, on the playground, in the cafeteria?

The goals of the observation are:

1. To describe the child's general behavior and how it relates to the criteria established in the DSM IV

2. To observe skills in a variety of areas to determine whether delays are present

3. To note any atypical behaviors that warrant more formal testing; for example, weak visual-motor skills noted in a writing activity

These observations form the core of basic information required to confer diagnosis and to begin to understand the actions of the child. Once the observational data have been collected, the teacher compiles them and presents a written referral to the appropriate party. This may be a supervisor or the child study team (or diagnostic team), who then initiates the assessment process.

A thorough assessment should include the following:

1. Clinical history

2. Parent interviews

3. Teacher interviews

4. Parent rating scales

5. Teacher rating scales

6. Psychometric evaluation

7. Tests of coordination and motor ability

8. Cognitive achievement testing, if appropriate, and language assessment if appropriate

9. Physical examination, including vision and hearing testing

10. Observation

In making the diagnosis of attention deficit disorder, the following components are to be examined:

1. The DSM IV diagnostic criteria

2. Interview information from parents and teachers, especially inferences as to the sources of difficulty

3. Scores obtained on rating scales (checklists)

4. Objective measures that document difficulty in cognitive areas requiring attention and planning

5. Available information from combined data indicating discrepancies among areas considered

Goldstein and Goldstein (1990, 96) suggest that "problems of attention disordered behavior should cause the child difficulty in at least 50 percent of school situations when making the diagnosis." The psychometric instruments that are part of the multidisciplinary evaluation are commonly administered by the school psychologist or the diagnostic specialist. Throughout the assessment, the practitioner should be keenly observant for difficulties with vigilance and sustained attention. On tests of vigilance particularly, students with ADD/ADHD appear impulsive and complete the tasks without planning. The practitioner will want to note the behaviors listed in Figure 5.

The multidisciplinary review involves history, observation, and parent and teacher questionnaires. The ability-achievement testing that is part of a complete review may include some of the following evaluative tools: Auditory and Visual Attention Span subtests of the *Detroit Tests of Learning Aptitude—Revised* (Hammill 1985); *Developmental Test of Visual Motor Integration* (Beery and Buktenica 1967); the Arithmetic, Digit Span, and Coding subtests of the *Wechsler Intelligence Scale for Children III* (Wechsler 1974); and the *Woodcock-Johnson Psychoeducational and Cognitive Batteries—Revised* (Woodcock and Johnson 1989).

The important factor is not which test is administered, but rather the child's response to the different and unique subtests. A skilled diagnostician compares vigilance, impulsivity, sustained and focused attention, and selective and divided attention during all measures and provides an impression concerning the degree to which attentional factors influence performance and personality style.

The classroom teacher is asked to observe behaviors and record them on a checklist. A variety of teacher rating scales have been used with children who have ADD/ADHD. Figure 6 represents a summary of some of these rating scales.

There are more than 42 different rating scales available to assess children with attention deficit disorder. These checklists help assess vigilance, attention, hyperactivity, and performance. The daily documentation teachers can provide to both the physician and the multidisciplinary team by completing observational checklists is an important part of the assessment process. The checklists can also be used when discussing different behaviors with parents. It is always helpful to have another professional observe the child and compare observations with the teacher in order to provide an overall review of behaviors.

The school nurse is a particularly valuable member of the team process and can be an excellent observer using this checklist format. The nurse's training in recognizing normal growth and development, as well as in observing and recording behaviors, makes this professional an important part of a collaborative effort. Often the physician will ask a nurse to use the checklist during a therapeutic trial period of a medication. The nurse helps evaluate the effects of the medication by gathering observational data—such as before-and-after documentations of behavior—and by observing the child for side effects. Once a physician has established the dosage using the checklist as a guideline, the preceding measures can be taken less frequently, based on input from the physician and parents.

In most cases, a child with an attention deficit disorder does not qualify for special education services after the multidisciplinary evaluation. Dr. Larry Silver (1989) estimates that only 20 percent of the attention deficit population also has a concurrent learning disability. This means that most children with an attention deficit disorder will be educated in the regular classroom. They may, however, be eligible for services under Section 504 of the Rehabilitation Act. This provision will be more thoroughly described in Chapter 2 and is an important part of understanding the educational intervention for a child with an attention deficit.

Figure 5

- Does the child impulsively answer questions (or select answers in forced-choice formats) without appearing to think about alternatives?

- Does the child fidget even when appearing interested in the task?

- Does the child's conversation appear random or sound like a "free flight of ideas"?

- Does the child look away from the task in response to noises or visual distractions? Does the child comment on external noises or objects in the room that are unrelated to the task at hand?

- Does the child frequently ask questions such as, "When will this be over?" "What's next?" or "What other things can we do?"

- Does the child yawn after activities requiring sustained attention?

- Does the child doodle in class or draw on hands, sneakers, and other things?

- Does the child stare off into space or appear to be "glassy-eyed"?

- Does the child lose papers, assignments, books, and the like?

- Are the student's desk and backpack messy and disorganized? (Jones 1991)

- Is the child able to stay alert during tasks requiring sustained attention?

- Does the student appear to lack persistence?

Figure 6
Observational Checklists

- *Academic Performance Rating Scale* (DuPaul, Rapport, and Perriello 1990)

- *ADD-H Comprehensive Teacher's Rating Scale (ACTeRS)* (Ullmann, Sleator, and Sprague 1985)

- *Attention Deficit Disorder Scale* (McCarney 1989)

- *Child Attention Problems Checklist* (Edelbrock 1988)

- *Revised Child Behavior Profile, Teacher Report Form* (Achenbach and Edelbrock 1983)

- *Conners' Teacher Rating Scale* (Conners 1989)

- *Levine Selected Attention Scale* (part of the ANSER Questionnaire Form; Levine 1985)

- *Teacher Observation Checklist* (Goldstein and Pollock 1988)

- *Yale Children's Inventory* (Shaywitz 1987)

Chapter 2
The Role of the Classroom Teacher or Education Professional

When working with an ADD student, avoid punishing statements such as, "When will you remember your homework?" or "Why can't you remember your pencil?" Instead, redirect with understanding: "How can I help you to remember your homework?" and "Let's think of a way to help you remember to carry a pencil."

Model, create, show the ADD student what works. After all, that's what we do best as teachers—teach.

—Clare B. Jones
New Teacher Workshop
San Diego Unified School District
September 1992

I believe that the role of a classroom teacher is literally that of an "environmental engineer," one who arranges the learning environment for the child's success and who encourages learning through that environment. The teacher has the opportunity to provide children with ways to express their ideas and participate in social and emotional experiences. Through this interactive participation, the student begins to develop adaptive and independent living behaviors. It is critical for classroom teachers and other educational professionals dealing with children who have attention deficit to know exactly what an attention disorder is and how it differs from other learning problems that we might see in the school environment.

When I am doing workshops, one question I am often asked is, "How can I tell if this child is lazy or if he has an attention deficit disorder?" I am discouraged by that question because I fear that the person asking does not regard children as the individuals they are. If we accept that all individuals learn in different ways, we can see why we, as professionals, must approach learning with a variety of techniques. The "environmental engineer" sets up the environment in the classroom so the child will learn, knowing that students who have the most firmly established knowledge base are the ones who can most easily assimilate and apply new information and grow.

We accept that all children learn, but we also know that they may learn differently. Therefore, the challenge before today's education professionals is to understand what an attention deficit disorder is, to understand normal development of attention, and to begin to set up strategies and interventions that allow this child to benefit from the educational environment (see Figure 7).

Figure 7

The Role of the Classroom
Teacher or Other Interventionist

1. Know and understand what an attention deficit disorder is.

2. Know what the normal course of attention development is.

3. Use checklists to help support your observations of the student.

4. Have another professional observe the student with you, using an identical checklist.

5. Collaborate with team members to provide the best accommodations for the student with ADD/ADHD.

6. Identify the student's strengths.

7. Employ behavioral interventions and educational techniques to best meet the student's needs.

How can one person effectively individualize instruction for all students? Materials are one key. Cooperative learning activities are another. Effective strategies are a third. These three keys, employed by an aware teacher, can make a difference for all children.

Just as there is no magic pill to cure an attention deficit disorder, there is also no magical strategy that will change this child's life forever. Rather, it is a cluster of good, strong teaching techniques that balance theory and practical application which will make the difference. What I have compiled in this book are a variety of strong teaching interventions and strategies that seem particularly appealing to the child with an attention disorder but, in fact, will work with all children. They are simply good teaching skills and principles.

My hope is that in seeking out special instruction for the child with attention deficit, educators will read this book and realize that to be excellent environmental engineers, they must apply sound teaching techniques, and that the answer to serving the child with attention disorders in the classroom is *the answer to serving any child in the classroom.*

Understanding the Strengths and Weaknesses of Students with an Attention Disorder

So often when we look at the characteristics of attention deficit disorder, we tend to look to the weaknesses or the areas we perceive as dysfunctional. We need to understand first what the child's strengths are to be able to constructively compensate for or alter the weaknesses. This way, we can take what the child does well and use it to help him or her cope with the weaker areas.

Strengths in Children with ADD/ADHD

I have noted that strengths in children with attention disorder vary—just as individuals vary—but they tend to cluster in some basic observable characteristics, which are listed on the next page:

20

Visual gestalt skills. Visual gestalt is simply the ability to see the "big picture" quickly. Children with this strength see the whole picture, "the cover on the book," and quickly determine what has occurred or what will occur. They quickly interpret others' feelings by their expressions and body language and often react based on that immediate impression.

Long-term memory. Children with this particular strength are often able to recall particular events and unique experiences that occurred years before. Parents report that their child may recall unusual occurrences from months ago and report them accurately. One mother related to me a story involving her daughter. As they drove by an office building one day, her daughter said, "Mom, there's that building where we saw that lady wearing the silver boots. Remember? We stopped here to see Aunt Connie, and she was in the lobby." That incident had occurred two years prior!

Recently, I observed one of my clients in school and heard him say to his teacher: "Mrs. Smith, you wore that cowboy blouse last year to the basketball assembly. I saw you when I was in second grade."

Creativity, inventiveness, imagination. Children with ADD/ADHD often have particular creativity with great imagination. They are able to describe events with intense emotion and vigor. Their oral descriptions of how they lost their homework assignments can excite an audience! Parents and teachers are impressed with the multitude of their ideas and the range of their responses.

Unusual application of higher-level skills. Often observed in mathematics applications, this ability to quickly integrate simultaneous thinking is a definite strength. The child may miss basic calculation steps but understand the higher application process of the problem.

Verbal expression. Another strength for these students tends to be verbal expression skills. They can speak at length about a topic, freely adding other subjects to the initial topic as they speak. Their conversations can be exciting, multifaceted, and dynamic.

Challenges for Students with ADD/ADHD

Conversely we must also examine some of the areas which challenge these children. Although they have the capacity to see the big picture quickly (whole gestalt), they overlook the details and sequential steps of a task.

While their conversation is engaging and lively, they may not listen to others' conversations. They appear almost egocentric—more interested in their own conversation than in others'.

Their long-term memory skills enable them to develop a background of cumulative events, but their short-term memory skills are weaker and make day-by-day tasks more difficult. They can remember everything you want to know about the history of Nintendo, but they can't remember to put their names on their papers in class.

They are challenged by work that is rote, tedious, or sequential in nature, that requires detail or careful scrutiny. They bore easily. Yet they are often compassionate, curious, and most enthusiastic about areas where they have been successful.

As teachers, we must learn to take their weaknesses—"the lead" in their lives—and help them turn them into "gold" (strengths). Figure 8 may help us see their strengths and weaknesses as a balance, not as a detriment. When we understand the balance of these strengths and weaknesses, we will be able to design curricula and learning activities to serve children's needs.

Figure 8

Typical Strengths and Weaknesses of Children with ADD/ADHD

Strength	Weakness
Verbal expression	Listening
Quick application of skills	Poor planning and organization
Visual gestalt	Visual detail
Long-term memory	Short-term memory
Intense emotions	Impulsive
Enthusiastic, curious	Bored easily
Active	Impatient
Generalization of ideas	Written expression of ideas

Affective Skills

Children with ADD/ADHD will learn more successfully when the adult's body language quickly interprets meaning for them. Body language involves eye contact, body carriage, facial expression, gestures, and certainly physical proximity. Effective body language gives students immediate feedback and communicates what the adult is expressing. Therefore, children with attention deficits will do better in a learning environment where the adult has strong physical mannerisms that reinforce her or his behavioral limits.

For children with an attention deficit, making eye contact is often difficult. Because they are so easily distracted, they are always looking at a variety of things, and they find it difficult to look at one thing. Conversely, they can be looking right at you, making eye contact, without listening at all to what you are saying! Therefore, skilled teachers will allow their eyes to sweep the room continually and, as they do so, glance directly into the eyes of individual students. It's helpful to stand in the general proximity of the student who tends to be looking around and finds it difficult to focus on the teacher. Strong facial gestures—such as a wink, "the look," a frown, a smile—and physical gestures—such as "thumbs up," pointing a finger, putting a hand on one hip, standing up very straight—can also add to this visual message.

> Remember this: The least effective way to correct a child with an attention deficit disorder is verbally.

Three Principles of Instruction

Three principles are critical when working with children who experience attention difficulties: *brevity, variety,* and *structure/routine* (Jones 1989). By integrating these concepts into lesson planning, you can design activities that will best serve students with ADD/ADHD.

Brevity. Attention and concentration are greatest in short activities. Frequent brief drills or lessons covering small chunks of information will result in greater learning.

Variety. Children with attention difficulties tend to perform more poorly on the second presentation of a task because they are hindered by what one researcher calls "flagging attention" (Douglas 1983). A child with attentional problems who perceives an activity as repetitive or "boring" will have difficulty staying on task. By presenting the same material in slightly different ways or with different applications, you can maximize students' attention.

Structure/Routine. A consistent routine, enhanced by a highly organized format to activities, will provide a focused environment for easily distracted children. Specific daily schedules that include well-planned experiences with smooth, well-defined transitions from one task to another are optimal for these children. Rules, expectations, and consequences should be clearly stated and specific.

Variations of these interventions will be helpful for all students and should enhance the learning environment. How well these principles will improve the potential of students with attention deficits only time and continued research will tell. We need strategies that are valid and reliable. As we begin to employ the techniques suggested by research, we will begin collecting our own data. Through conscientious planning, professionals can provide experiences for children with attention difficulties that will enhance and support their individual development while offering variety and challenge.

Normal Development of Attention

We need to begin with a thorough understanding of the normal development of attention and its implications for learning. In my first book (Jones 1991) I shared the information in Figure 9, taken from Cooke and Williams (1987), which outlines the six levels of normal development of attention, based on Jean Reynell's research. These levels are important for all education professionals to understand and may be used to effectively assess the child's development of attention skills.

Figure 9

The Levels of Normal Development of Attention

Level 1 (birth to 1 year)
Level 1 is characterized by extreme distractibility, when the child's attention flits from one object, person, or event to another. Any new event (such as someone walking by) will immediately distract the child.

Level 2 (1 to 2 years)
Children can concentrate on a concrete task of their own choosing, but will not tolerate any intervention by an adult, whether verbal or visual. These children may appear obstinate or "willful," but in fact their attention is single-channeled, and all extraneous stimuli must be ignored in order to concentrate upon the task at hand.

Level 3 (2 to 3 years)
Attention is still single-channeled in that the child cannot attend to auditory and visual stimuli from different sources. A child cannot listen to an adult's directions while playing, but whole attention can be shifted to the speaker and back to the game, with the adult's help.

Level 4 (3 to 4 years)
The child must still alternate full attention (visual and auditory) between the speaker and the task, but now does this spontaneously without the adult needing to focus that attention.

Level 5 (4 to 5 years)
The child's attention is now two-channeled (that is, the child understands verbal instructions related to the task without interrupting the activity to look at the speaker). Concentration span may still be short, but the child can be taught in a group.

Level 6 (5 to 6 years)
Auditory, visual, and manipulatory channels are fully integrated and attention is well established and sustained.

Reprinted with permission from page 34 of Cooke, J., and D. Williams. 1987. *Working with Children's Language*. Tucson, AZ: Communication Skill Builders. Originally published in 1985 by Winslow Press, England.

24

Children who are developing normally are believed to expand their attention spans as they relate and respond to information within their environment. The ability to demonstrate persistent concentration over a period of time is dependent upon intact cortical and subcortical brain functions (Mirsky 1978). The hypothesized neurological component of attention deficit may be the factor that interacts with or impedes concentration and attention.

Researchers now recognize that there is often a strong genetic history of poor concentration in the families of children with attention disorders. At times, it is very difficult for an adult to comprehend that a child who is fidgeting, demanding attention, and impulsive may have a physical, inherited disorder. The inattentive student is often described as "lazy" and "not motivated." Education professionals want to know how to spot the difference between a child with attentional problems and a child who is "just difficult." Some of the problems these children are experiencing within the classroom are a result of the disorder. And just as surely, some of the ways they react are due to the fact that they have learned to respond to the way they have been treated.

The Referral Process and the Rehabilitation Act

In most schools, once a teacher has observed a child for a period of time and feels concerned about the child's needs, he or she will refer the child to a teacher assistance team (TAT) or child-study team for further discussion. The first step in a TAT would be to share information regarding the child's strengths and weaknesses as observed by the teacher. The TAT generally consists of interested faculty, special education faculty, and a counselor or consulting psychologist. As a first step, the team suggests additional alternative strategies to the referring teacher. The teacher returns to the classroom to implement these techniques. If, after a designated period of time, the teacher feels that the student is continuing to struggle, the team reconvenes and may invite the student's parents to join the session. At this time, a referral may or may not be made for further evaluation by the diagnostic team.

Understanding Section 504, the Rehabilitation Act, and How it Serves Students with ADD/ADHD

Most students with an attention deficit disorder do not qualify for services under IDEA, the Individuals with Disabilities Education Act (formerly the Education of the Handicapped Act). If the student has a definite learning disability, or qualifies for any of the other handicapping conditions noted under IDEA, that student is then eligible for related services as provided by 94-142. There are other students who are not eligible for IDEA services but who nevertheless are deemed handicapped under Section 504, and to whom a school district may therefore have responsibilities. IDEA defines as eligible "students who have certain specified types of impairments and who, because of those conditions, need special education." Section 504, in contrast, protects all students with disabilities, defined as those having any physical or mental impairment that substantially limits one or more major life activities (including learning). Section 504 of the Rehabilitation Act of 1973 covers all students who meet this definition, even if they do not fall within the IDEA-enumerated categories and even if they do not require a special education program.

Students with attention deficit disorder may not be covered by IDEA. They will, however, be protected by Section 504 if, because of their attention deficit, they are substantially limited in their ability to function at school and are considered handicapped within the language of Section 504. Section 504 prohibits discrimination against persons with disabilities—including both students and staff members—by school districts receiving federal financial assistance. Thus, in order to fulfill its obligation under Section 504, a school district has a responsibility to avoid discrimination in policies and practices regarding its personnel and students. The school district has specific responsibilities under the act, which include the responsibility to identify, evaluate and, if the child is determined to be eligible under Section 504, to afford access to appropriate educational services.

If the parent or guardian disagrees with the determination made by the professional educational staff of the school district, he or she has a right to an impartial hearing. Every school district should have designated one administrator as the 504 coordinator.

What Does 504 Guarantee the Student with ADD/ADHD?

1. A free and appropriate education, including individually designed instruction
2. A written plan
3. Reevaluation before significant changes are made in placement
4. Accommodations within the regular classroom

The school typically will develop a written plan describing the handicap under 504 and the accommodations or, if needed, related services that will be provided. The plan specifies how the regular program and related services will be provided and by whom. In making such a determination, the school study team considers all available relevant information including comprehensive assessments done by the school's diagnostic team, background history provided by the parents, observations, and background documentation including standardized testing. The parent or guardian is involved in all of the child-study meetings and decisions regarding accommodations. When a plan for providing services and accommodation is developed, all school personnel who work with the student are informed of the plan.

In 1991, the State of Arizona Department of Education devised a series of topical papers on Section 504 entitled "A Challenge for Regular Education." These guidelines, a collaborative effort of five authors, are provided to every superintendent, director of special education, and assistant superintendent in the state. An Accommodation Plan and a sample Notice Form from that book are reprinted in Figures 10, 11, and 12.

Figure 10
Notice Form

_____
date

Dear Parent or Guardian:

This letter is to inform you that there is a concern about how your child is progress-
ing in _____ school. We have attempted
some accommodations for your child and wish to arrange a meeting to discuss further accommodations in order to ensure that _____ is
afforded access to an appropriate education. We have scheduled a meeting on
_____ at _____. This meeting will be held at
_____ to discuss your child's
educational needs, and we would very much appreciate your participation.

If you have any questions, or if this meeting time is not convenient for you, please
call me at _____. We will discuss your questions or arrange a
mutually convenient meeting time.

Sincerely,

Name and Title
cc: Student's Cumulative File

_____
Reproduced with permission of Arizona Department of Education, 1993.

Figure 11
Student Accommodation Plan

Name: _____

Date of Meeting: _____ Date of Birth: _____

School: _____ Grade: _____

1. Describe the nature of the concern:

   _____

   _____

   _____

2. Describe the basis for the determination of disability (if any):

   _____

   _____

3. Describe how the disability affects a major life activity:

   _____

   _____

   _____

4. Describe the reasonable accommodations that are necessary:

   _____

   _____

   _____

   _____

   _____

   _____

Review/Reassessment Date: _____
(Must be completed)

Participants (Name and title)

_____ _____

_____ _____

_____ _____

_____ _____

_____ _____

cc: Student's Cumulative File
Attachment: Information Regarding Section 504 of the Rehabilitation Act of 1973.

Reproduced with permission of Arizona Department of Education, 1993.

Figure 12

Sample Completed Student Accommodation Plan

Name: Jay Wong

Date of Meeting: 10/4/94   Date of Birth: 9/26/80

School: Cactus   Grade: 8

1. Describe the nature of the concern:

   Jay does not return his homework assignments. Although they are often completed, he does not hand them in. Jay has great difficulty arriving in class on time and is unprepared for class, often arriving without pencils or paper.

2. Describe the basis for the determination of disability (if any):

   Jay was diagnosed two years ago as having a severe attention-deficit/ hyperactivity disorder.

3. Describe how the disability affects a major life activity:

   Jay's multidisciplinary team indicated he has great difficulty with daydreaming and short-term memory. He is failing three classes because he has not returned homework. He is failing one class (gym) because he never has his gym suit.

4. Describe the reasonable accommodations that are necessary:

   Jay will move into the special organizational homeroom, where homeroom teacher will collect all assignments before classes start. All teachers will give homeroom teacher Jay's assignments one week in advance. Jay will receive one copy, and one copy will be mailed to his parents. Parents will provide a box of pencils and paper for each class teacher so Jay always has enough materials in each room.

Review/Reassessment Date: December 3, 1994
(Must be completed)

Participants (Name and title)

Jay Wong	student
Kathy Shafer	homeroom teacher
Julie Fenyk	gym teacher
Jim Rosenburg	principal
Sarah Murphy	social studies teacher
Katie O'Connor	art teacher
Kristin Trehan, Ph.D.	school psychologist

cc: Student's Cumulative File
Attachment: Information Regarding Section 504 of the Rehabilitation Act of 1973.

───────

Reproduced with permission of Arizona Department of Education, 1993.

Accommodations That Might Be Suggested in a
Written Plan for Students in the Regular Classroom

- Modified assignments (shorter tasks, breaking activities down into small chunks)

- Special assistance from professionals, counseling, monitoring of medication

- Reduction of written or copying tasks

- Alternative testing methods

- Use of compensatory tools in the classroom—for example, calculators, hand-held spellers, tape recorders, computers, carbon copies of notes

- Advance notice of due dates for assignments

- Outline of class discussion. Outline of key vocabulary words

- Supplementing verbal instructions with visual information

- Use of peer tutor

- Copies of notes on a chapter provided directly to the student

- Modified textbooks or workbooks

- Provision of an extra book for at-home use—one book stays in the classroom, the other stays at home

- A buddy phone system of names to call when not sure of assignments

- A "direction helper" in class who has a copy of the directions the teacher has presented; student reviews information with the helper

- Note-takers, consultation with special resource personnel

- Modification of nonacademic time, such as lunch, recess, and physical education

These accommodations can help a teacher in setting up suggestions and interventions in the classroom. These accommodations will be referred to again in the chapters covering elementary grades through high school.

For a full copy of the memorandum on Section 504, call your local office on civil rights or the Federal Office on Civil Rights, Washington, D.C. (202) 732-1635.

Figure 13
Section 504 and ADD/ADHD: The Steps to Success

Is the student considered "handicapped" under Section 504?

If *yes* then:

1. Student has a physical or mental impairment that substantially limits one or more major life activities.

2. Student has a record of such impairment.

3. Student is perceived as having such an impairment.

If *no,* then:

1. Maintain documentation that includes the names of team members who made the decision and their qualifications for doing so.

2. Maintain the original evaluation data.

3. Retain records of placement options that were considered.

4. Notify parents in writing of decision.

Proceed to:

1. Determine whether special services or classroom accommodations are necessary (IDEA considerations).

2. If special services are ruled out, specify interventions, accommodations, and adaptations to be considered in present placement.

3. Determine whether student has access to a free and appropriate public education.

4. If the student is eligible for special education services, determine the least restrictive environment (LRE).

5. Develop an accommodation plan.

6. Put the plan into action.

7. Review the plan.

ADD Plus an Additional Handicapping Disorder

Some students will be eligible for services under federal law 94-142 if they qualify as having an eligible handicapping condition in addition to attention deficit disorder.

Judy Schrag, former director of the Office of Special Education Programs, has indicated that when a multidisciplinary team meets to design an individualized educational program (IEP) for a student who has attention concerns in addition to another condition, ADD will be secondary, and the student must qualify for services due to the primary disability (Schrag 1992). The IEP should address the primary disability and provide accommodations for the attention problems. Dr. Schrag stated that one member of the multidisciplinary team must have specific knowledge of how to identify and treat the disorder. Schools do not have to consult physicians when outlining special education services for children with attention deficit disorder.

Top 10 Questions Teachers Ask Regarding ADD/ADHD

The following ten questions were taken from workshops I have presented for teachers. They represent the questions typically asked by teachers.

Q: How can I help just one child in the room at a time? I have 30 children in my class. I can't just stop for one.

A: This answer is twofold:

a. The techniques for handling children with attention deficit are simply good teaching skills—all children will benefit from these strategies. Avoid using them selectively for just one student.

b. You are not the only teacher in the room, nor are you the only model in the room. Children learn from their peers, from visuals you employ in the lesson, from what they read, and certainly what they do and experience in the classroom. You are the environmental engineer—you facilitate the environment, the experiences, so the students benefit and learn. Make use of all these things when you plan your days, and you will quickly realize you are not the only "teacher" in the room.

Q: When I do something for one student—for example, reducing a weekly spelling list to half the words, I don't feel I'm being fair to the other students. How can I handle this?

A: First understand the distinction between fair and equal. Try this statement: *"Fair is helping you to do the best you can with the techniques I have. Equal is treating everyone the same."* To illustrate how absurd the comparison between fair and equal is, think of telling a child with hearing aids: "Remove your aids during this listening test. I must treat you equally. It is not fair for you to have amplified hearing."

The master teacher starts the year by labeling and anticipating these behaviors. He or she lets the class know from the first day that accommodations will be made for individuals in the class. Example: "If John needs an accommodation that you don't, I want you to know John will have that opportunity in this class. Just like

I will offer you every strategy you may need when you are struggling. My goal in this class is to help all of you learn. If that means John gets 10 words to your 20, so be it. We all work together, but we all learn differently. The question in this room is not 'How did you learn?' but 'How well did you learn?'"

You can further encourage this healthy respect for individuals by choosing library books to read to your class that typify children who have had challenges and met success. This technique, called bibliotherapy, uses literature to illustrate to your students that they are more alike than different.

Q: How do I know the difference between attention deficit and just plain lazy?

A: When this disorder exists for a child, it's a totally encompassing situation. It doesn't occur just in your room, but everywhere in this child's life—at home, at play, at church or temple, in the shopping center, at the movies, etc. Every child with attention disorder has a long history of difficulties. Talk to other teachers in this child's daily life, to parents, to past teachers. Gather data. For the child with an attention deficit, you will see a history of teacher and parent comments regarding this child's behavior. There is a reality to this disorder, and it has not escaped observation by others in the child's life.

Q: How can I motivate the child with ADD?

A: How do you motivate any child? You find what interests him or her and use it as a factor in your instruction. We know that all children respond to strong visual hands-on presentations in school and opportunities to be leaders, "in charge," "in control." A dynamic classroom, with a skilled teacher who is genuine in his or her presentation and provides opportunities for student feedback, can light this child's internal spark.

Q: If I teach the student with ADD only one skill, what should it be in your opinion?

A: List making! Teach the child how to list tasks and then cross them off as they are accomplished.

Q: Does medication make this child smarter? The children I have seen on it are getting better grades.

A: Extensive research on the effects of Ritalin before and after test-taking experiences demonstrates no significant changes in scores. Slight differences were observed in handwriting and in completion of details. My guess is that, with medication, these children are more focused and will review work more thoroughly before handing it in, will "hear" and remember all directions prior to doing the task, and will be less impulsive when working. As a result, the quality of their work improves. They now begin completing tasks they failed to complete before; therefore, their grades improve.

Q: Why is there a greater incidence of boys with attention disorders?

A: Development researchers such as Helen Bee tell us most physical and neurodevelopmental disorders have a higher prevalence in males. Her research indicates that this is due, in part, to the fact that male and female babies differ at birth in several ways:

    a. Girls are more mature physically at birth.

    b. Girls are more reactive to several types of stimulants at birth.

    c. Girls tend to have a higher level of fat cells at birth, which can be protective in common birth situations. At birth, boys tend to have a thinner myelin sheath (the protective coating around individual nerves). Although the sheath develops later on, and boys "catch up" to girls, their nervous system may be more vulnerable to insult.

In addition, we are now becoming more sophisticated at identifying girls with this disorder. Girls tend to have less of the hyperactivity factor, and thus are harder to diagnose early on.

Q: How long will the child be on medication?

A: That varies on a case-by-case basis. The attending physician, parents, teachers, and child are all part of the observation team. The manufacturers of stimulants recommend periodic discontinuation of the medication. During these periods, the observation team compares notes and makes recommendations regarding continued usage. It is a team decision, and the student's input is extremely critical.

Q: Are there successful adults with attentional problems?

A: Absolutely! Every one of us knows a creative, successful adult who has experienced struggles with attention, memory, or hyperactivity, but who has found a challenging and successful career. The research on adults is limited, because only in the past five years have research studies begun to examine adults with ADD/ADHD. But there are many well-known people with this disorder who have been successful, including actor Dustin Hoffman and photographer Ansel Adams.

Q: I think I can help this child in the classroom, but what can I do to help his parents? They are struggling!

A: There are now hundreds of support groups for families across our country. The two largest parent organizations are:

    Ch.A.D.D.
    499 Northwest 70th Ave., Suite 308
    Plantation, FL 33317

    and

    A.D.D.A.
    8091 South Ireland Way
    Aurora, CO 80016

Suggest that parents contact these groups for further information regarding materials and local parent meetings.

Chapter 3
Behavior Management Strategies

> We are waiting. . . . We are waiting for Justin. . . . We are still waiting for Justin. Everyone wants to hear this story but Justin. When he can show me he is ready to sit up, we will start. We are waiting. . . .
>
> —Teacher's comments to a student with ADD
> observed in an elementary classroom

Behavior, as defined in *Webster's Dictionary*, is a "form of nervous, muscular, and emotional response of an individual to internal or external stimuli." In contrast, misbehavior is a term used to describe a behavior that is inappropriate to the situation in which it occurred. The very difficulties children with attention problems experience often result in behavior that some educators feel is inappropriate for the school setting. These behaviors include, but are not limited to:

- fidgeting, tapping, playing with objects

- talking to self while working independently

- rocking, tipping the chair back, frequently leaving seat

- calling out in class

There are many interventions to help education professionals manage or cope with these challenges on a daily basis. This section will include a brief review of a variety of behavioral strategies and highlight some techniques which may prove helpful for the student with ADD/ADHD.

According to well-known psychologist Sam Goldstein, the research literature indicates that about 80 percent of the daily interactions children with attention deficit disorder have with parents and teachers are negatively reinforcing. No wonder they appear unmotivated and discouraged! A typical day for this student includes comments such as, "Will you please stop moving in your chair?" "Stop that tapping with your pencil!" "If you won't stop moving, we're going to have to ask you to leave the room." "When are you going to learn to walk in the hall?" "I'm looking at you, and I am expecting you to look at me."

Comments like this begin to erode the child's self-esteem. Therefore, we must begin to look at the behavior of the child with an attention deficit in an *investigative way* and ask ourselves, (1) does this behavior fit the descriptors of the disability (for example, inattention, impulsivity), or (2) is this behavior noncompliance? Being able to discriminate between the two—inability to control versus noncompliance— will help us in our management of this child. Here are two examples illustrating the difference between these two situations.

Example 1. Justin is working at his desk on a paper-and-pencil activity requiring some cutting and pasting. Justin has managed to knock over the glue several times, he turns and snips at other children with his scissors, he drops papers on the floor, he moves things back and forth, and he gets up from his desk several times. Mrs. James, his teacher, comes over and says, "That's it, Justin. You can't work independently. I'm taking these things away, and you're not going to be able to finish the project."

Justin is a child with attention-deficit/hyperactivity disorder. What she just observed was difficulty with impulsivity, poor control of that impulse, difficulty with small muscle activity, and visual motor integration difficulties. A more appropriate response would have been for the teacher to come over and suggest that Justin clear his desk, work on one activity at a time, and not bring over the glue until he's ready to go on to the gluing activity. She could reward Justin for on-task behavior and place a capable student model next to him, so he can imitate some on-task behavior and coping skills in the activity. In this way, Mrs. James would be responding to the situation by using her abilities as a specialist to train, organize, and demonstrate planning skills, rather than selecting punishment as a response.

Example 2. David is standing at the back of the line as his class is waiting to go into an assembly. David continues to bother his neighbors. Finally, his teacher says, "David, if I have to ask you again to stop bothering your friends, I will request that you step out of line and sit on the rug for a while." David continues to bother the other children, and the teacher says, "David, I'm going to have to ask you to step over here for a bit." David strikes out and says, "Don't touch me. I'm not going to move. You can't boss me, nobody bosses me."

This is an example of noncompliance. Now is the time for the teacher to employ whatever consequences are appropriate. Perhaps David's difficulties with impulsivity caused the problem, but his response was one of noncompliance. How could David's teacher have avoided this situation?

One way is to anticipate trouble spots throughout the day. Waiting in line can be tedious for all children; therefore, planning ahead and involving difficult students in other activities during this time might eliminate this problem. Having David run an errand at that time or letting him go get a drink of water to give him a break would have been a stronger teaching strategy. In the Activities for Elementary Grades are suggestions for some brief learning activities that can be used to fill waiting time (see pages 76-77).

Throughout the literature, physicians and psychologists often recommend to teachers that the child with attention disorders needs one-on-one attention. The reality is that very often this child is served in a classroom situation of 25 to 1 or more. As I suggest behavioral strategies in this chapter, I will take the following realities into account:

1. You are managing a group. You are not working with one or two students, and generally suggestions about working one-on-one are not an option.

2. Your goal is not to be the most important personality in this child's life, but rather to be the person who sets up the most academically successful situations. As Brophy and Good (1974, 32) state, "What the teacher does in the classroom rather than his/her personality is what increases student achievement." This is the inspiration for the model I will be presenting here.

3. You need to understand cultural differences and use that information to discipline all children fairly.

4. Understanding attentional difficulties and what types of behaviors they induce will help you deal with the reality of this problem.

5. Remember, all behaviors have a payoff of some kind—attracting attention, gaining power, expressing hostility toward those we do not like, or being left alone (Dreikurs, Grunwald, and Pepper 1971).

The Use of Reward

Because children with ADHD have such difficulty inhibiting the types of behavior that easily promote negative responses—such as fidgeting, talking, squirming in their seats—it is paramount for the adult to be thinking of positive ways to reward and work with these children.

Children with an attention deficit can't easily regulate either their moods or their actions, largely because they are not aware of them. Therefore, we need to provide ongoing and supportive feedback. When these students are learning new skills, it's important to give a great deal of positive reinforcement. This technique, *behavior shaping*, refers to gradually changing a person's behavior by reinforcing even the smallest movement toward the desired goal while ignoring inappropriate behaviors.

1. Be specific rather than general in your praise. Examples of specific praise are:

   • "You answered five out of eight right."

   • "The way you just handed the game pieces to Bob shows me you know how to play nicely. It's wonderful that you can cooperate in this game."

   • "Wow! Three out of three right! You studied hard, and it paid off."

2. When you praise the child, emphasize the effort, not the quality of the outcome. Examples of this are:

   • "I bet you worked hard on that one."

   • "The way you wrote your name at the top shows me you took time to write this paper."

   • "You really learned a lot about dinosaurs. Thanks for telling me."

   Avoid general comments such as: "Nice paper" or "I like it."

3. Your praise should emphasize the feelings of the student, not your feelings and reactions. Rather than saying, "I'm so proud of you," an example of emphasizing the student's feelings might be:

   • "Nine out of ten! I bet you feel wonderful!"

   • "You got a B on that paper? You must feel proud of yourself."

4. Avoid valuative praise such as:

   • "You were so good at the assembly."

   • "You can really behave when you want to."

5. Express your feelings of appreciation without words that evaluate the student's behavior. An example might be:

   • "I enjoyed working with you today. Thank you for entering quietly."

6. Honest recognition without value judgments about students' personalities allow you to recognize effort and show appreciation, while letting students make their own evaluations about themselves. When you describe your own feelings or describe the efforts of your students, the praise is productive, as in this example:

   • "It makes me feel good to see such quality work. I know you must feel proud of this paper. The amount of work that's gone into this math paper is obvious."

Positive reinforcement is regarded by many researchers as perhaps the most potent technique for modifying voluntary behavior. In his book, *Toward Positive Classroom Discipline*, Harvey Clarizio (1976, 20) states, "Positive reinforcement has two basic functions. It facilitates the acquisition of new behaviors and it maintains behaviors once they are acquired." When using positive reinforcement, one must consider these basic questions:

1. How often should a reward be given?

2. When should rewards be given?

3. What types of rewards should be given?

Look for the Positive

Be a "detective for a day." In trying to approach a child from the positive direction, try the following suggestions:

Instead of dwelling on the problems the child has, try to discover the child's talents, likes, dislikes, and abilities:

- Find out what the child already knows.

- Ask others what skills the child already possesses.

- Ask parents: "What does your child like, what is she [he] interested in?"

- Ask the child: create a personal interest survey and ask the child to complete it.

Take a note card and at the top write these words: "Friendliness, Wisdom, Sense of Humor, Love of Routine, Honor, Favorite Items." As you observe the child throughout the day, try to focus on these words. Jot down any example of the child demonstrating these things on the card.

Note on the card what messages are on this child's T-shirt. (Children often select T-shirts that feature heroes, favorite rock groups, vacation places, and so on.)

This card system forces you to look at the positive and interesting aspects of the child's life for one day. Once you have identified a list of qualities, go to work highlighting them. Shift your focus away from what this child *can't do* to concentrate on the abilities, the assets, the advantages this child has.

Reward Attending Behavior

When you observe the student working on a task and appearing focused and involved, jot down your specific observation. When the activity is over, go immediately to the student and comment on the on-task behavior you noticed. Examples:

- "Josh, when you were taking notes from the encyclopedia, you were right on task—eyes on book, quietly writing. Well done! You know how to take notes."

- "Lindsay, during independent silent reading you were really involved with your story. I could see how much you were concentrating when I looked over at you."

Regular rewards help a student to "catch on" to new behavior, while occasional rewards help the student to "hold on" to behaviors already learned. Possible rewards are suggested in Figures 14 and 15.

Figure 14
Suggested Rewards for Elementary Students

1. Listening to stories or music on a tape recorder or phonograph with earphones.

2. Working in an art corner with special paper scraps and pieces of art materials.

3. Audiotaping a story for the class to listen to.

4. Being first in line.

5. Leaving class early for lunch.

6. Taking charge of a variety of activities, such as attendance taking, passing papers.

7. Getting a drink at any time without asking permission.

8. Being allowed to clean the chalkboards and erasers.

9. Arranging the toys on the game shelf, and being the first to pick a game to play.

10. Going to the library to work on a special project relating to a unit being studied.

11. Taking important messages to other teachers' rooms or to the office.

12. Tutoring a younger child in school.

13. Calling on students in the classroom. (Turn to the student and say, "Your turn to pick a student.")

14. Being able to look at magazines, special seasonal books, sports programs, etc., that are collected in a certain area in the room.

15. Being allowed to help the office secretary, custodian, cafeteria worker, or librarian for a 15-minute period.

Figure 15
Suggested Rewards for Middle School and High School Students

1. Using a computer.

2. Doing extra-credit problems as an opportunity to raise grades.

3. Making up questions to appear on an upcoming test.

4. Choosing the display to go on a bulletin board.

5. Challenging the teacher or another student to a mind game, such as *Racko*, chess, or a computer game.

6. Reading magazines in a corner of the room.

7. Listening to selected tapes on a tape recorder.

8. Appearing as a guest lecturer in other classes.

9. Doing special crossword puzzles that involve math skills.

10. Solving mystery problems involving situations that require application of math skills.

11. Being dismissed early from class in order to work in the office.

12. Audiotaping a story for a student who is having difficulty reading.

Physical Proximity

Adults can use physical proximity to control a student's behavior without ever having to use verbal correction. Frederick H. Jones, in his book *Positive Classroom Discipline*, talks about the power of physical proximity. He suggests that teachers who need to deal with misbehavior move near the offending student, establish brief contact, and say nothing. The student will usually return immediately to proper behavior. To use physical proximity effectively, Jones says, the teacher must be able to step quickly alongside the target student. He feels that body carriage and posture can very effectively communicate authority. Children with an attention deficit quickly "read" body language and benefit from immediate feedback regarding whether the adult is uninterested, positive, angry, and so on.

Jones also suggests that experienced teachers employ a variety of hand signals to encourage and discourage behavior and to maintain student attention. Examples he gives are palm out (stop), palm up and flexing fingers (continue), finger to lips (quiet), finger snap (attention), thumbs up and a wink (approval). These gestures are effective ways to communicate to the child with an attention deficit without using unnecessary verbalization.

Response Cost

Response cost has been an effective behavioral strategy. It is particularly effective with students who need more structure and routine. In response cost, students are rewarded for positive behavior with tokens or points, and they lose their tokens for undesirable behaviors.

Examples of Response Cost

1. Mrs. Shafer is concerned because during a five-minute whole-class review at the end of the day, Justin continually interrupts the discussion and rarely raises his hand when he wants to take a turn. She decides to use a response cost technique. Knowing Justin likes to be the first one out the door, she uses that as a reward. She talks with Justin privately and briefly discusses the five-minute review at the end of the day, stating in a positive way, "I know you have good things to share, but others want to have a turn as well." She suggests a strategy to help everyone have a chance to share. "I'm going to hold a clipboard, and on it will be five lines. Every time you shout out or interrupt during the review, I will cross out one line on the clipboard. (The clipboard remains private, and only the student and teacher know what is on it.) If there are any marks left at the end of the period, I will call on you, Justin, to be first excused. If there are no marks left, you will be the last."

   As in any good behavior modification system, Mrs. Shafer will continue to use the program daily. After some time, she will reduce the number of lines from five to four, announcing this positively to Justin. "It's great that you can do this, you have only four lines now on the chart. You must feel so in control."

   If this approach begins to lose its appeal for Justin, she adds an element of surprise. One day, she hands Justin a new pencil and states, "You really know how to raise your hand. Thank you for working so hard." Eventually one day she can "forget the clipboard" and just use facial gestures to monitor this situation.

2. Demory is in a second-grade class. During independent reading time, he is constantly out of his seat. Mrs. Beck wants to help him stay seated for one five-minute period, so she sets up the following response cost plan with him. Five squares of red paper will be taped on the front of Demory's desk. Every time he leaves his desk during the five-minute work time, he will lose one square. If, at the end of five minutes, he has any squares left, he will then have a predetermined reward. If there are no squares left, no reward will be given.

Adults can positively direct response cost through verbal affirmation. For example, in the situation above, if Demory looks like he is starting to get out of his seat, the teacher can positively direct him and reward the entire class by saying:

> We have so many good workers in this class. I can look around the room and see people who know what to do and they must be proud of themselves. I see Demory, I see Amy, I see Carol; all are trying very hard to work at their desks.

This cuing in advance of misbehavior is a positive and specific way to let the student know you understand he is trying to stay in his seat and win the reward.

Group Response Cost System

A useful behavior management technique during independent work time is a group response cost system (Salend 1990). In this technique, group behavior rather than individual behavior is monitored. Students are divided into predetermined teams or groups. At the beginning of the work period, each team is awarded an equal number of tokens. Token boards or charts are placed in full view of students on the wall or on an overhead and within easy access of the instructor. The instructor removes a group's token (or checks off a mark on the overhead) each time a group member displays an inappropriate behavior. If any tokens or marks remain at the end of the time period, the predetermined reinforcement (for example, ten minutes of free time) is given to the entire team. A cautionary note is in order here. Do not allow one child to become the scapegoat for the group. Eliminate the group competition if this begins to occur.

The Super Kid Award for Elementary Students

This is a special award placed where all students can see it. At specific times during the day (such as during a whole-class learning activity) the instructor displays the award. While it is in place, students can earn points or tokens that can later be exchanged for reinforcers. A certain amount of time is designated for this activity. The time interval required in order to receive a token is gradually increased as the class demonstrates success. Eventually, when the class understands the system, student members can assume responsibility for removing the award.

This technique loses its effectiveness if it is used daily. It is most helpful when in special situations, such as a day of particularly difficult transitions or a special assembly day.

Student Self-Management to Increase On-Task Behavior

Several researchers have implemented self-management strategies to reduce problem behavior, increase on-task behavior, and increase academic success in a variety of subjects. Research indicates that student self-management can have a number of benefits. Overall, self-management strategies increase students' responsibility for their own learning and behavior. Specialists in self-management believe that it can heighten students' self-esteem while reducing demands on the teacher's time. The Council for Exceptional Children provides a research brief for teachers (Brief T3, March 1990) that gives suggestions for self-monitoring. It includes the following information:

1. First establish a cuing system to let students know when they need to self-monitor. Some systems are turning on a tape recorder or raising a hand or making marks on the chalkboard. The time between the cues should be randomized, so students cannot predict when the monitoring time will occur. For children with attention disorders, the time intervals should vary and should be shorter than two minutes.

2. Identify the behavior to be monitored. For example, in a class of 10- to 16-year-old students who are not able to complete their daily work without supervision, the behaviors to be monitored were "paying attention," and "not paying attention." Paying attention was defined as doing the assigned work. Not paying attention was defined as doing anything other than the assigned work—for example, talking, looking around the room, drawing, or cleaning one's desk.

3. Design a recording sheet and hand out copies to all students (see Figures 16 and 17). The sheet should contain spaces for the student's name, a question asking whether the expected behavior is being performed (example, "Was I working?"), and columns for "Yes" or "No."

4. The students need to know why they are working on self-monitoring, and it should be presented as a cooperative way of making the class successful.

5. After handing out the recording sheets, it is important to ask the class to participate in role playing what might be acceptable behavior and what might not be. For students with attentional problems, modeling and role playing are very effective. During the role plays, the adult should actually participate as if she or he were also a student. This way, students have an additional

model to observe before beginning to monitor their own behavior. It is important to review the self-monitoring procedure briefly after holidays and weekends. This review can be an excellent way to track the students' progress and evaluate whether the self-monitoring helped increase on-task behavior.

6. Then explain what the signal will be for students to mark on their recording sheets whether or not they were paying attention. You might set up at the back of the room a tape recorder that will periodically play a tone, raise your hand at a certain time, or make a mark on the chalkboard at random times.

One excellent self-monitoring tape and manual is produced by Dr. Harvey Parker. Reasonably priced and well written, the program is available through the ADD Warehouse; 300 N.W. 70th Avenue, Suite 102; Plantation, FL 33317; (800) 233-9273.

Figure 16
Sample Self-Management Task Card

The student determines at the end of a specified time as announced whether he or she was on task. Student determines the number of points based on a predetermined scale.

Name _____ Week of _____

Was I working?

Points	Monday	Tuesday	Wednesday	Thursday	Friday
Total Points					

10 points = Effort
20 points = I am improving
30 points = *Awesome!*

My goal is to get _____ points by _____ (day).

43

How to Introduce Self-Monitoring on an Individual Basis

1. On a one-to-one basis, talk openly with the student about the behavior you are hoping to monitor.

2. Positively introduce self-monitoring as a "new" strategy that will help him or her begin to be able to self-manage the inappropriate activity.

3. Ask the student to describe the expected behavior. If age appropriate, have the student model or role play the appropriate behavior.

4. Introduce the strategy to the student.

   Example: "Doug, here is a self-monitoring check sheet. Every time you hear the beeper, record whether you were or were not paying attention. Place a check under the column that fits your attention at the time."

5. Practice with the student.

6. Put the check sheet on the student's desk when class begins.

7. Meet with student to review tally marks.

Sometimes in a large class the beep technique described previously can be annoying to others in the class. To ameliorate that irritation, you may want to consider:

- Using it only in small-group situations.

- Having the student use earphones when using monitoring tape.

- Wear a watch with a beeper and casually raise your hand or give some other signal that only the student is aware of.

Figure 17
Self-Monitoring Sheet

Name _____

Date _____

√ = on task when beeper rang

O = off task

Monday	Tuesday	Wednesday	Thursday	Friday
O√√√O √√√√				

Total √ = _____

Total O = _____

Mnemonic for Listening Skills

Another strategy that may be helpful for children with attention deficit is the use of a mnemonic or clue during a large-group activity. Jeanne Bauwens and Jack Hourcode, associate professors at Boise State University, developed a technique called "The Listening Strategy." They used the word LISTEN as a mnemonic device to help students with attention deficits remember strategies to improve their listening skills. The teacher instructed each student to listen, and then wrote on the board the key words:

L = Look

I = Idle your motor

S = Sit up straight

T = Turn to me

E = Engage your brain

N = Now

Visual reinforcement was provided by listing the six listening instructions on a 3" x 5" card on each student's desk, as well as on a poster at the front of the room. Initially, the teacher paused after saying each step out loud, but as the students gained familiarity with the procedure, these pauses were minimized and ultimately eliminated.

After giving students the complete list of instructions on several occasions, the teacher reduced the amount of assistance by saying "listen," and then pointing to the six steps. These verbal prompts were then reduced further, with the teacher saying only "listen" and quietly pointing to the acronym on the card or poster. Eventually the teacher was able to simply say "listen," and the students reviewed the acronym quickly, silently, and independently.

The results of this technique in a classroom situation showed that all students consistently attended more effectively to oral instructions. It seemed to decrease the number of times the teacher had to repeat information, and it seemed to decrease student frustration over mistakes caused by misunderstanding instructions.

A Classroom Token System

A classroom token system provides an overall management approach for an entire classroom. It is similar to response cost, in that students earn or lose points for behaviors. Unlike response cost, which usually targets one behavior to be changed, this system awards points to the class for a selected list of behaviors. The tokens or points are later exchanged for activities, rewards, objects, or privileges. A positive approach is to give points for things that are accomplished. Children with attention deficits also require some penalties, however, so it is probably most helpful to build this into the token system: removing tokens should be contingent upon inappropriate behavior or failure to meet the guidelines of the behavior program.

Some teachers have set up rather complex systems (involving, for example, mock savings accounts with passbooks where children can record and keep their tokens and points) and have found such systems very successful. Because of practical constraints and the complexity of token systems, however, most teachers use them only to manage certain periods of the day.

The token system can also be used in a cooperative learning or group situation where the children earn rewards not only for themselves, but for their peers as well. An advantage to this situation is that under normal circumstances peers are often attracted to children who are off-task and will turn to them and reinforce the inappropriate behavior. Setting up a system where the group participates in the student's reward decreases the likelihood that peers will attend to inappropriate behavior.

For an in-depth discussion of the development of a classroom token economy, see Abramowitz and O'Leary (1991).

Ignoring and Redirecting

Whenever possible, ignore fidgeting, wiggling, tapping, and the like. Provide opportunities for purposeful movement. For example, if John continually taps his pencil on the table, you might respond by asking, "John, would you mind getting me the book over on the library table, please?"

Allow the child to hold something when working. Suggestions include a piece of crushed tinfoil, a miniature Koosh® ball, a small rubber ball, or a paper clip. I have observed that many students with ADHD concentrate better when they can finger some object.

Children with ADD/ADHD exhibit certain behaviors that tolerant adults should ignore. Some children develop habits such as tapping their fingers, wiggling their feet, or humming. Others use the same phrase over and over again, whine, or nag. By ignoring the behavior, you are not rewarding it. Sometimes you can redirect the child from a negative action to a positive one. Here is an example of redirecting a child's attention to a positive behavior:

Student: I want gum!

Teacher: Jason, look at the wheels on this truck. One is not turning.

Student: I want gum! I want some gum right now!

Teacher: Look, Jason, this wheel stays still when I push.

Student: Gum! Gum! Gum!

Teacher: Jason, I need you to push the truck wheel. Can you fix this?

With this question, teacher puts the truck into Jason's hands. Jason looks at the truck and begins to examine it (Jones 1989). Influential group leaders can also be a part of this modeling situation.

Contracting

The use of contracting, making a written agreement between the teacher and student, can be a helpful behavioral tool with students. A contract typically outlines the behaviors and consequences of a specific behavior management system (see Figures 18 and 19). The main benefit of contracts seems to lie in facilitating communication between the student and teacher or in the process of negotiating the contract. The student observes during this process that good behaviors "pay off" and that negative consequences accompany inappropriate behavior. Students with ADHD often complain of feeling "picked on" by teachers, and a contract situation conveys a sense of control. Students who negotiate a contract feel they have a greater voice in implementing a plan to modify their behavior. Self-direction and self-management skills may also improve through a contracting system.

For the child with an attention disorder, consider the following components in drawing up the contract:

1. A statement of the exact behavior that the student is to increase or decrease, defined in observable terms

2. A specific description of the reward and who will provide or implement it

3. Specific circumstances under which the behavioral goals will be met

4. A time frame for the length of the contract

5. A renegotiation clause in case of an unforeseeable circumstance (for example, school is closed unexpectedly for several days)

6. A bonus clause; that is, a special opportunity that may be included at your discretion (This appeals to the ADD/ADHD student's need for variety.)

7. Date and signatures of all parties

Figure 18
Example of a Group Contract

We ___(students' names)___ in Chemistry 109 agree to put our equipment away after class every day during the week of May 16.

I ___(teacher's name)___ agree that if the above contract is fulfilled, I will provide (5 minutes at the beginning of each class for students' social interaction at their tables. I will not start class until the timer indicates 5 minutes of free time is over.)

Bonus: _____

_____

Teacher: _____ Date: _____

Students: _____ Date: _____

_____ Date: _____

_____ Date: _____

_____ Date: _____

Figure 19
Example of an Individual Contract

I _____Jeremy Smith_____ will follow the class rules in social studies class for

_____Monday and Tuesday, April 3 and 4._____

I will:
Participate in class discussion by raising my hand.

I, _____Mr. Spencer_____, guarantee that if _____Jeremy_____ meets this goal, _____he will be

able to listen to the music of his choice during free period Wednesday. If he does

not meet the goal, he will stay after class for 30 minutes on Tuesday night._____

Bonus _____

_____

_____	_____
(Teacher)	(Date)
_____	_____
(Student)	(Date)

Changing Isolated Behaviors

To change isolated behaviors, the following steps are recommended:

1. Identify one behavior you want to change.
2. Require that behavior over a short period of time, so the child sees a beginning and an end to the time you are monitoring.
3. Observe the child frequently before setting up the schedule so you know, on average, how many times the child produces that behavior.
4. Have an immediate response between you and the child so that the child sees the consequence of that behavior in action.

Disruptive Behavior

Some students can be quite volatile and may initially refuse negative consequences (such as refusing to go to time out). In such a case, set a kitchen timer for a brief period (one or two minutes) after the refusal has occurred. Explain that the student can use the time to decide whether she or he will go to time out voluntarily or whether a more serious consequence must be imposed. Several experienced teachers report that this method successfully reduces the extent to which they have to physically enforce negative consequences with students and seems to "de-escalate" the situation. They emphasize that it is important *not* to give the misbehaving child attention or eye contact during the "decision interval," but rather to continue conducting class as normally as possible (Braswell and Bloomquist 1991).

Quick Tips

Here are some quick tips to add to your collection of behavioral management techniques.

- Avoid having long lines of students waiting for you at your desk. Place one chair by your desk and designate it as a "waiting chair." Post a rule that states if a child is in the chair waiting to talk with you, others must remain in their chairs until the waiting chair is empty.

- If students are working independently, and you are walking around the room grading or checking work as they complete it, have each student place a red square on the desk or stick a colorful shape on the side of the desk when they finish. This way, they can move on to other tasks, placing their finished work to the side for you to pick up and check.

- Collect colorful and unusual pens. When students are working independently and you observe a student to be off-task, walk by and say, "Carol, try this pen for a while. I like it, see what you think." This will add variety to the task for the student and provide you a positive way to correct behavior.

- When you assign daily or weekly helpers in your room include a "Direction Helper." After you have given directions for a group activity, give the helper a copy of the directions. Children who did not hear or understand your directions may go to the Direction Helper for one-to-one clarification.

- Because they are impulsive, children with attention disorders often hand in papers without checking them over for errors. If you suggest that they return to their desks to check their work, they often sign the paper and then bring it back in the same form. Instead, give them a definite plan. For example, you might state, "I see four wrong in this row. See if you can find them." This gives them a specific direction to follow, and they are more apt to complete the task.

- Make laminated cue cards for directions you use on a regular basis (see page 51). One example would be directions for writing headings on papers. Place the cue card on the desk of a child who needs additional reinforcement.

- Provide a *routine* for returning papers. Have a "Homework Checker" in each row or at each table. Homework Checkers collect students' homework at their table or row and write down on a specially placed note pad the names of students who did not do homework.

- Sometimes after you have given directions, a child will immediately ask you to repeat them. Try the 2 T's technique. Post the technique on a cue card.

Time to Talk: The 2 T's

1. When you get your paper, look it over and see if you can understand how to do it.

2. Place a T on the top of the paper if you don't.

3. Look one more time; if you still don't understand, place another T on your paper.

4. When you have two T's raise your hand.

5. That lets me know it's "Time to Talk," and I'll come right away.

Examples of Cue Cards

Heading

1. Name on paper

2. Date under name

3. Class period

Independent Reading Time

1. Choose a favorite book.

2. Find one (1) place in our room
   to read.

3. Read to yourself until assigned time
   is over.

Math Worksheet

1. Put name on paper.

2. Do two rows (you pick which ones).

3. Raise your hand.

4. I will check work.

5. Go to step 2. Start again.

Chapter 4
What Works? Approaches for Elementary School

I think I have radar ears. I can hear what's going on inside my classroom and what's going on outside, too.

—A 9-year-old boy with ADHD

More children are diagnosed with attention disorders during the elementary school years than at any other time. In fact, because of the high number of children who were not identified until they actually entered elementary school, some observers felt that attention deficit was primarily a reaction to formalized school instruction. As researchers investigated attention deficit more thoroughly, however, it became quite evident that the difficulties of the disorder were apparent long before formal school experiences.

Why, then, do students have more difficulty with the disorder when they enter a full-day normal school situation? The ability to succeed in school depends on one's ability to maintain sustained attention, attend to multistep directions, and work independently. The symptoms of attention deficit disorder let us know that these are exactly the parameters that will challenge children with this diagnosis.

Once educators understand the nature of the diagnosis (Chapter 1) and their role with the child (Chapter 2) they can begin to consider adapting instruction to meet the child's needs. Interventions can be selected that will help the student to begin to function more effectively within the school setting. The child study or teacher assistance team can offer a supportive and collaborative approach to designing strategies and accommodations.

Modifying the Classroom Environment

Although individual children vary in their ability to selectively ignore stimuli, many teachers have found that classrooms free from extraneous auditory and visual stimuli are most suitable (Telzrow and Speer 1986). The complete removal of distractions is *not* warranted, however. Reducing the degree of stimulation aids in focusing attention, but removing all distractions does not help these children significantly (Jones 1991). In fact, some evidence suggests that such efforts are counterproductive (Douglas and Peters 1979).

I observed a teacher lecturing to a group of second graders. Directly in front of the teacher was a very active 7-year-old who was fidgeting with a rubber band. As the teacher continued talking to the class, she reached over and removed the rubber band. Within seconds, the student began fingering a paper clip. She removed that, and a large eraser appeared. Frustrated, the teacher cleared the child's desk *and* his pockets! She gamely continued her verbal lesson. The child, undaunted, reached over to the neighboring student's desk and picked up a pencil to manipulate! The active child with ADHD appears to be *internally* distracted and can lose concentration in even the most sterile of environments.

Seating Arrangements

The role of classroom seating arrangements has never been examined specifically for children with attention deficit disorder. It has, however, been examined with regard to normal youngsters. Apparently, seating arrangements do have significant impact on rates of off-task behavior.

Teachers will often say to me, "If I could put every child who has difficulty in the front row, they'd all be in the front row." Therefore, one of the most successful classroom arrangements is a "U" shape (see Figure 20). Larry Liberman, in his work in the Boston City Schools, found that the U shape was an effective way of enabling students to imitate the strongest role model in the room, which is the teacher. Students have the benefit of physical proximity, in that they are all within easy reach of the teacher. In the U shape, the teacher will have more time and energy to look at each student without having to walk around or turn or stand behind some students in the classroom. The teacher is in direct view of all students. Because students with ADD/ADHD tend to have strong visual gestalt skills and respond well to visual modeling, the U-shaped seating arrangement seems an ideal way to help these children in the environment of the classroom.

Clustered seating has often been advocated in cooperative learning. In this arrangement, several children share a table or sit with their desks facing one another, which certainly helps in facilitating social interaction but impedes on-task behavior during independent seat work. The child will look at the other children at the table, as well as at other things in front of him or her. This can be highly distracting. I recommend starting the year with the desks in a U shape and, as students learn your style of teaching and the behavioral expectations in your room, gradually move to the group seating arrangement.

When students are in clustered seating, be sure that if you need students to turn and look to you for a direction, you stand directly in front of the students with ADD/ADHD. They will be the last students to turn and look at you in class. Therefore, avoid wasting time by waiting for them to turn; stand in front of them instead.

Placement of the Student in Small Groups

I often ask classroom teachers where they place the most difficult child in a small group. They typically respond, "Right next to me where I can keep an eye on that child." The fact is, you're not keeping your eye on the student in that location! When you turn to correct the student, he or she sees the side of your face. Then on looking up, the student is looking into the faces of the other students. They may make faces at the student, and that's the behavior that is modeled, not your suggestion. Whenever you can place this child so he or she is looking directly at you, you *will be more successful!*

Figure 20
Examples of Seating Arrangements

30 Students

ADHD

The U—23 Students

ADHD

ADHD   ADHD

Multiple U-Shapes

ADHD

ADHD

At the Reading Table

C   C   C

T   >   <   ADHD

C   C   C

ADHD = Place child with ADD/ADHD here.

55

Seating Strategies for Individual Work

When walking around the room, make sure that you do not stand behind a child and look over his or her shoulder to give instruction or correction. Instead, stand in front of or beside the child's desk so you are face-to-face.

Because some students may perform better in different settings, it can be appropriate to offer a student with ADD the opportunity to complete a seat-work assignment on a rug-covered floor rather than at a desk. Students who move frequently and have difficulty organizing their papers should be given a clipboard where they can mount and secure their work (Jones and Jones 1986).

Another alternative is to allow the student to straddle the chair horseback style, with the back of the seat across the student's chest. It is more difficult to tip a chair in this position, and it offers the child some variety in seating after a long period in one position.

Yet another strategy is to provide the student with a second seat in addition to the regularly assigned one. When you note the child tipping and moving in the seat, use a predetermined nonverbal signal (for example, tapping one finger on student's desk) to signal that the student may stretch, get up, and move to the empty chair. Sometimes, this brief break and change in location can be all that's needed to help the child focus again. Beanbag chairs are a great furnishing for a reading corner or study area in the classroom. Their shape conforms easily to the student's shape and seems to eliminate some activity.

Desks

Some students are challenged by the actual desk available in the class. One young man told me, "I was doing fine last year in my class when I had a desk with a top on it. But this year, my desk has an open bin on the side for books and papers. I can never find anything in it, and I am always touching something in it because it is right in front of my eyes!"

His teacher helped him out by turning the open bin side of the desk toward her. When he needs a book, the teacher reaches in and gets it for him. Pencils and erasers are kept in a plastic box in the desk, and he is permitted to "finger" a Koosh ball as he works.

Some teachers have found that their students prefer having a desk with the chair attached. This makes tipping the chair back virtually impossible.

Some schools report success using tables rather than desks. In classrooms where tables are used, materials such as pencils are kept in a designated area. Students each pick up a pencil when they enter the room and deposit it as they exit. Students are given one book that remains in the classroom and one book that remains at home. Books are stored in the classroom and are collected daily by assigned helpers in the class. In this situation, some of the clutter in a desk is eliminated and routines are established for organizing materials that are used daily.

Organizing Classroom Materials

Students who are disorganized and have difficulty with planning are more successful in a room that offers orderly routines for storing materials and supplies. Labeling and storing materials in an efficient way so students can find them easily is essential (Lund and Bos 1981).

Color coding can be an excellent way to organize materials. Color codes can be used to indicate categories, content, level of difficulty, or other relevant dimensions.

Color code your materials to match the folder or book used for each class. For example, if the math book is red, store materials related to math in boxes marked with red. (Colored adhesive dots can be an easy way to color code materials.) Extend the color coding from your storage into your planning. Continue the "red-is-math" theme by providing a red box where only math papers are returned. When writing homework assignments on the board, place a red circle or red check next to the math assignments. Use red clips to organize math papers that are graded and need to be returned.

Transitions

Transitions from one period to the next and within a class period make up approximately 15 percent of the school day (Rosenshine 1980). Disruptions in the normal daily routine and moving from one area or topic to another are challenging for children with ADD.

Difficult times for students with ADD in the daily routine will be moving from informal activities (recess, walking through the hall, free time) to formal classroom activities (reading independently, seat work, listening to another person read). As the class moves from unstructured to structured activities, you are likely to observe that the student with ADD is more distracted and more apt to be talking with or bothering classmates. Students with ADD handle transitions more successfully when they can go from focused to unfocused, formal to informal, structured to unstructured activities (see Figure 21).

Planning activities or cues to aid transitions will be helpful. Employ auditory or visual cues to signal changes in the routine or breaking points in an activity. For example, with younger students, a song sung daily to signify the end of free time marks this transition. For older elementary students, you could use clapping to the beat of a rhyme (where you begin and students join in), or you could have a visual cue card that you place on the overhead projector at transition time.

As students return from an unstructured activity, it is helpful to present a transition activity before beginning a structured task (see Activities for Middle School and High School, pages 116-19 for suggestions). On returning from recess, the students can spend some time sitting informally in groups and reviewing flash cards from an earlier math lesson. This is followed by passing out books, and then by a structured independent reading time. This example offers a way to gradually make the transition from unstructured to highly structured activities. The key is to examine your schedule and coordinate activities so they follow this pattern.

Sample schedule

- Short free time in centers
- Reading period
- Recess
- Flash card review of new words in game format
- Reading workbook

Avoiding abrupt transitions will produce calmer, more organized changes.

Figure 21
Transition Tips

Transitions are more successful when students can go from:
• Focused to unfocused activities
• Formal to informal activities
• Structured to unstructured activities

The *most* difficult times for students with ADD will be transitions from:
• Informal to formal activities
• Unfocused to focused activities
• Unstructured to structured activities

Visual Cues

Capitalize on inattentive students' need for visual information to support verbal instruction by offering visual cues as you present information. Employ an overhead projector, erasable board, chalkboard, or standing easel to offer visual explanations that supplement your verbal descriptions.

The following visual graphics are suggested:

1. Draw webs or maps of main ideas as you present them.

2. Use graphs or other visual representations to illustrate contrasts or differences in quantities.

3. Highlight material you put on the board using color, if possible, to emphasize specific points or areas to be remembered.

Children with attention problems tend to perform poorly on tests of visual motor integration. So, not surprisingly, they often have difficulty copying material from the chalkboard to paper or from a book to paper. They are likely to copy material from the board or a textbook letter-by-letter, often skipping words, instead of reading word-by-word, retaining each word, then writing it. Numbering each row of written material helps students return to the correct place more quickly. Or add lines, boxes, and squares to the text to be copied. Students with ADD will remember the visual differences on the board rather than the words they are copying and will look for a specific drawing rather than a word to cue them where they left off. I have heard my students say aloud to themselves, "Now, where was I copying? Okay, yes, by that line." They were using visual cues to return to work—not their memory of the text.

Here is an example of visual cues that might help students copy a poem from the board.

1. As I walked to school today

2. I saw so many things along

3. the way.

4. A puppy barked hello as I

5. walked by.

6. My feet walking fast, my

7. ↑ head in the sky,

8. I watched the (clouds) and to the

9. (sun) said hello.

10. I passed the houses of |friends|

11. I know.

12. A bird sang a song just overhead.

13. A robin I saw with a breast

14 of red.

15. Soon I was at |school,| such a

16. happy sight.

17. I wonder what I'll see when 👁

18. I walk home tonight!

Clare B. Jones

Charts that outline daily routines, graphs, or posters displaying math tables are other visual depictions which attract the child's interest. Many students with ADD can recall exactly what visual the teacher drew when explaining a subject but cannot remember the verbal description the teacher provided!

Verbal Cues

Challenged by poor attention for multistep structured questions, the child with attention disorders rarely gets all the verbal material presented. These students can often repeat verbal information word-for-word immediately after hearing it, but the next day or a week later they have little integration of the thought.

When presenting complex or multistep directions, include the following elements:

1. Use key phrases to gain students' attention and focus them on the steps in the directions. Possible key phrases might be:
   - "Ready, set, look"
   - "Pencils up"
   - "1—2—3"
   - "Focus"
   - *"This* is important"

2. Use numbers or letters of the alphabet to sequence the steps of a verbal direction, just as you would do with written instructions. For example:

   • "One, put your name on the paper. . . . Two, circle all the nouns. . . . Three, put your pencil down."

Pause briefly after each step. Ask students to repeat directions for the entire class. Do not choose the student with ADD unless you are quite sure he or she knows each step and can answer correctly. Select stronger peer models for this exercise, children you know have heard the material correctly the first time. This avoids embarrassing the student who may have missed a step. Neither exposing a student's weaknesses in front of classmates nor putting a student on the spot is productive.

Reinforce your verbal message with an animated style and visual supports. If directions are very complex, have ready an individual written copy of the instructions with different steps highlighted in color.

Overhead Transparencies

A neurologist once told me that the overhead projector is the best piece of classroom equipment for helping a student with ADD. He felt this was because of its strong visual impact. I concur, and feel there is another reason for its importance. An instructor who is using an overhead generally faces the students. The students see the material, but the instructor is looking directly at the students. No backs are turned, no messages are given from the "side" of the face. The overhead projector allows the adult to face the students and monitor who is attentive and who is not.

When employing an overhead projector, use colored overhead transparencies to add variety and dimension to a lesson. Manipulatives can add interest—make use of small shapes, cut-out alphabet letters, numerals, and the like. All can be placed directly on the overhead and offer additional dimensions to your visuals. Students can also actively participate throughout the lesson by coming forward and writing their responses on the transparency. They can also copy what is on the overhead while at their desks.

Students should be encouraged to use overhead transparencies when they make class presentations or book reports. You can provide blank transparencies for students to use when preparing oral reports for the class.

Overhead transparencies can also be used as an aid in transition time. The following activity will appeal to students because of its personal interest. It is best used when students are returning to class after an unstructured time.

Make an overhead that asks questions about students' interests or personal characteristics:

   • What is your favorite musical group?

   • What group do you not like?

   • What is one song you heard recently that you really like?

   • What is one song you do not like?

or

   • What is your favorite television commercial?

   • Why do you like it?

Have students write their answers on a piece of paper. Then allow them one minute to share their information either with a partner or with you.

Additionally, the overhead can be used as part of a behavior management program. Place a list of students' names on the overhead. As you circulate about the room helping and working with the students, occasionally stop and place a point by the name of a student who is on-task and working well. At the end of the day, total the points and dismiss the students who have the most points first.

When students are particularly disruptive and talkative, turn on the overhead projector and begin writing the directions or steps to your next lesson. The overhead is a focus point that often serves as a strong incentive for students to get started on the new task.

Schedules

ADD students have difficulty with productivity—completing tasks, finishing work, and planning tasks effectively. They benefit from the instructor posting a daily schedule and reviewing it frequently. The schedule can be written each day on the chalkboard or on sentence charts or on an easel. Use color or shapes to designate different activities such as lunch or recess. This adds interest to the schedule and often encourages the reluctant learner to "tune in" to an activity that may have appeared tedious.

The schedule should be organized in such a way that there is a predictable format for the day, even though the specific activities within each designated time slot may vary. The schedule should include the time frame for each activity. When possible, each completed activity should be checked off as it is accomplished. Assign a different student each day to this responsibility. You may also want to provide some students with individual schedules to keep at their desks.

Rules

An important part of any learning environment is establishing rules in order to create an environment where academic and social growth are fostered. Rules set up the expectations for the environment and provide a routine to guide the interactions which occur within it. Research has demonstrated that the most important classroom behaviors can be covered using no more than five to seven rules. These rules must relate specifically to the needs of each setting.

For the student with ADD, rules need to be stated in a clear, concise manner. Whenever possible, rules should also be stated in positive terms. For example, "Raise your hand to speak," rather than, "No talking." Students are also likely to follow rules more closely when they are involved in writing them. Students can be asked to suggest rules, and then the class can review all the suggestions and select the final list of class rules.

Once the rules have been selected, involve the class in designing a neat, attractive sign upon which to display them. Place the sign in a prominent location in the room, then make sure students practice and recite the rules daily. You can help students learn the rules by using role playing and verbal description to illustrate the behaviors which make up the rules. Avoid reading the rules rote style. Instead, try these alternatives:

- "All the boys who followed rule 2 yesterday, raise your hand."

- "Table captains, read the rules to your table. Pick one rule to model for our class."

- "If your name starts with J, read rules 1 and 2 aloud."
- "Everyone who ate at a fast-food restaurant once last week, stand and read the rules to the class with me."

Throughout the day, reinforce the rules and "spot" students following them. Comment on your observations:

- "Sandy and Robin know how to follow rule 3, class. They always raise their hands to speak."
- "I like the way students at table 2 follow rule 1. They work at their table during free time."
- "The girls at the back of the room are doing a very good job with rule 2."

Picture cues can help elementary students recall the rules. In addition, actual photos of students modeling the rules can be placed on the poster or around the room as additional cues.

Modeling

Visual modeling and role playing are excellent ways to help students with attention deficits recall instructions and directions. When you introduce a lesson, have one or several students act out or actually do the beginning steps of your direction. Employ strong student models to act out or role play such things as the proper way to pass books out, sharpen pencils, or raise hands. A major component in the success of a classroom is using positive models. Students are highly reinforced by peers, and using peer models can result in quicker task recall.

Photographs can add to your modeling efforts within the room. You can use pictures of your students to show sequential instructions. When a student has difficulty remembering an instruction or procedure, he or she can review the photo sequence.

- Take a photo of every student in the group. Place strips of hook-and-loop fastener (such as Velcro) on the back of each picture. At the end of a day, feature students' pictures on a prominent reward bulletin board covered with fabric. Write a card for each featured behavior—for example, Most Cooperative, Most Courteous, Friendliest. Place one child's picture next to each card.
- Photograph students modeling desired behaviors, such as returning materials to their proper places. Then let students review the appropriate photos before they start an activity. Post the photos as reminders when the activity is underway.
- Photograph a sequenced activity routinely done within your setting (for example, working on the computer during free time). Photograph each step of the sequence of booting up and using the computer. Students can then review the photo steps before they choose the computer work area.

Color Cues

The effectiveness of using color to draw attention to relevant discriminative stimuli has been well documented (Zentall and Kruczek 1988). Color can be helpful when it is used to enhance a task, not distract from it. Add color accents to key features of repetitive tasks that children find unmotivating. Color cues can be added to written work, worksheets, and study sheets.

- Highlight structural parts of words students are beginning to learn. Emphasize multisyllabic words or compound words in color.

- Have students place information they are learning in color-coded categories (for example, all nouns on blue flash cards, verbs on yellow; see the sample Subject-Verb Agreement Worksheet in Figure 22).

- Highlight sounds students are having difficulty with. For example, if a student is having problems with a blend in a word, color only the blend.

- Highlight areas on worksheets where multiple directions make the activity more complex. This will help the student differentiate among the separate parts of the worksheet (see the sample Pronouns Worksheet in Figure 23).

- Have a student highlight key words as you read directions on a worksheet together.

Figure 22
Typical Worksheet #1

Agreement of Subject and Verb

The subject and the verb of a sentence have to match or agree. If the subject is singular, the verb must be singular. If the subject is plural, the verb should be in its plural form, too. Remember: a **verb** ending in s is **singular,** but a **noun** ending in s is **plural.**

One girl **runs.**

Two girls **run.**

Each of the following sentences has a singular subject and a singular verb. Rewrite each sentence to make both the subject and verb plural. The first one has been done for you.

1. The table needs repair. __The tables need repair.__

2. The cat sits on my dresser. _____.

3. The dog barks loudly. _____.

4. The creek floods in monsoon season. _____.

5. An elephant never forgets. _____.

Typical Worksheet #1 Highlighted in Color

In the worksheet below, shading has been used to represent colored highlighting markers.

Agreement of Subject and Verb

The subject and the verb of a sentence have to match or agree. If the subject is singular, the verb must be singular. If the subject is plural, the verb should be in its plural form, too. Remember: a **verb** ending in s is **singular**, but a **noun** ending in s is **plural**.

One girl **runs.**

Two girls **run.**

Each of the following sentences has a singular subject and a singular verb. Rewrite each sentence to make both the subject and verb plural. The first one has been done for you.

1. The table needs repair. The tables need repair.

2. The cat sits on my dresser. _____.

3. The dog barks loudly. _____.

4. The creek floods in monsoon season. _____.

5. An elephant never forgets. _____.

Figure 23
Typical Worksheet #2

Personal Pronouns

Pronouns that are used as subjects of sentences or in place of predicate nouns are called subject pronouns. The subject pronouns are:

I   you   he   she   it   we   they

Pronouns used as objects, indirect objects, or objects of prepositions are called object pronouns. The object pronouns are:

me   you   him   her   it   us   them

Write the correct pronoun in each blank:

1. _____ (He / Him) and Kelly are in serious trouble.

2. John and _____ (I / me) are going to Disneyland on Monday.

3. The doctor gave _____ (they / them) some medicine.

4. _____ (She / Her) will be able to join the team.

5. The Phoenix Suns gave _____ (we / us) free tickets.

Personal Pronouns

① Pronouns that are used as subjects of sentences or in place of predicate nouns are called subject pronouns. The subject pronouns are:

I   you   he   she   it   we   they

② Pronouns used as objects, indirect objects, or objects of prepositions are called object pronouns. The object pronouns are:

me   you   him   her   it   us   them

Write the correct pronoun in each blank:

1. _____ (He / Him) and Kelly are in serious trouble.

2. John and _____ (I / me) are going to Disneyland on Monday.

3. The doctor gave _____ (they / them) some medicine.

4. _____ (She / Her) will be able to join the team.

5. The Phoenix Suns gave _____ (we / us) free tickets.

List Making

The child with attention deficits is challenged by sequential planning and organizational activities. List making is therefore an essential ingredient in daily success. By teaching list-making strategies, adults can be instrumental in helping this child "put order into a day."

In my workshops, I often ask how many of the participants are list makers. I am overwhelmed by the response. More than half the people will raise their hands!

I then ask a more selective question, "How many of you, if you make a list and then do an additional task that is not on the list, will write that finished activity on the list and cross it off?" Most list makers agree they also do this. I believe the reason for this is that list making is motivational. When you cross items off the list, you feel that you have accomplished something. Even though you have completed a task that is not on your original list, you may want to add it just to get that good feeling of "I did it! I crossed it off my list!"

Children with attention difficulties do not often get that satisfying feeling of task accomplishment. One of the criteria of their disorder is that they rarely complete tasks. List making can be an intervention that helps them begin to cope with this characteristic.

Start the student with making brief, short lists. Research indicates that short lists lead to faster mastery (Carmine 1990). Model list making in front of the class using your overhead projector. For example, "Let's make a list of what we need to do in this social studies lesson. As we finish each task on our list, we will cross it off."

Competency in list making eventually leads to goal-setting skills. In the advanced grades, teachers have reported that students with ADD/ADHD have difficulty setting priorities. A start in list making at the elementary level can be a building block for tasks at a higher cognitive level later on.

Manipulatives

Research has verified the success of students using manipulatives in learning tasks, particularly in mathematics. The inattentive student often is more focused on a task that incorporates an active response and, hence, responds well to the use of manipulatives. Teachers can offer counting cubes, chips, toothpicks, and the like as supportive tools in mathematics activities. The very active student may, however, become more unfocused if manipulatives are introduced in a disorderly manner.

Here are some suggestions for structuring the use of manipulatives:

1. Place each type of manipulative in a small, easy-to-handle container.

2. Limit the number of manipulatives presented.

3. Offer incentives for returning manipulatives to the container.

4. Place a cafeteria tray under the container and have the student work directly on the tray. This provides a sense of order to a rather unstructured activity.

If the child becomes very distracted, remove the original manipulatives and offer new ones such as number lines or number graphs. The student can then count by moving a finger along the line or graph rather than by counting objects.

Writing Challenges

"I hate to write!" is the cry of many children with attention problems. This dislike is probably due to the fact that many of them have delayed visual motor integration skills. When they start to copy something, they are usually distracted by something else, and so the task takes longer to complete.

Dr. Mel Levine (1987a) identifies these four writing problems in his book *Developmental Variation and Learning Disorders*:

Finger agnosia. Finger agnosia involves difficulty keeping track of where the pencil is during a writing task. These children are observed to put their heads very close to the page as they write in an attempt to "watch" the pencil.

Fine motor memory. Students with fine motor memory problems have trouble recalling memories for finger movements through the many different nerve connections between the hands and the brain.

Eye-hand coordination. Students with poor eye-hand coordination skills have difficulty getting their eyes and fingers to work together. They find tying shoes, finding small objects, and snapping or fastening objects challenging.

Dysgraphia. Dysgraphia is a neurological disorder involving the actual process of writing thoughts on paper. This student has great difficulty expressing ideas through writing or written symbols. There is no difficulty with verbal expression of ideas.

Inattentive children tend to have the greatest difficulty with the fine motor memory component. They begin to write and lose the thought they were going to put on paper. They are hurried; as a result, their writing looks rushed, almost primitive in style as they attempt to get the task over with.

To help students who struggle with writing, we need to focus on two areas: the physical and the emotional. On the physical side, there are many compensatory techniques we can employ to reduce their difficulties. Accommodations can be offered to help these students be more productive. On the emotional side, we need to let them know that the strategies they are learning will, in turn, make them "feel better" because they will be more productive and ultimately more successful. Strategy instruction informs students about cognitive tools that they can use to attain academic success. Without such instruction, many students would not discover the strategies at all or would do so only after a great deal of frustration and failure.

The first step in helping students with writing difficulties is to observe the actual pencil grasp. If a student is holding the pencil in an awkward manner, model a more comfortable and efficient grasp. Most children under 8 years of age will accept and benefit from some modeling of a different grip. Above the age of 8, in my experience, many children appear to find it too difficult to accept a new grip; they tend to return to their original form.

For students interested in changing their grip, commercially available plastic pencil grippers may be helpful. Other students can improve their pencil grasp if they use their third and fourth fingers to hold a small sponge or crushed wad of tinfoil or paper in the palm of their hand as they write.

Writing Tools

In the early childhood years, we recommend large chunky chalk, big crayons, and 1/2" thick pencils. We know the muscles in the hand are not completely formed until about age 7, so younger children will benefit from larger writing tools.

As children get older, they will enjoy using all types of writing tools. Let the student experiment with a variety of pencils and pens. Poor writers often pick the finest pointed instrument they can find; they like the crisp line it produces. Students who grasp the pencil tightly and press hard do better with the fluid movement of a lightweight ball-point pen.

Try inexpensive mechanical pencils (disposable type). Although some children are flustered initially because the lead breaks easily, others find them faster and more comfortable to use.

These pencils produce a clean, fluid stroke when writing, and some children find them easier to hold because of their textured plastic coating.

Have parents send a box of pencils to school for each student at the beginning of the school year. Collect pencils and encourage students to add to your collection. Have a box designated just for pencils. Students can deposit pencils there as they leave.

A clipboard can also be helpful for these students. The firm surface makes writing easier, and the clip holds the paper in place. This is especially helpful for very active students who push their papers around as they write.

Paper

Several years ago I was working with a client who had retinitis pigmentosa, a hereditary eye condition from which she will eventually go blind. Her physician suggested she write on pastel colored paper, especially in rooms where the lighting creates a glare on white paper. This suggestion has been successful for other students as well. By reducing glare for students as they write and adding some variety, pastel paper colors can make the task more enjoyable. Studies have also found that children who have writing difficulties tend to do better on paper with narrow lines than with wide-ruled paper, because the former requires less execution.

Writing Interventions (Physical)

When students are practicing beginning writing skills, have them use both the index and middle fingers to spell or write letters in the air, using whole-shoulder movements. This brings a stronger kinesthetic sense into the task.

When teaching writing strokes, use verbal mediation skills to help the student remember the task. Students may benefit from verbal input accompanying tasks like letter formation that have very similar rote presentations. (Example: "When we make the letter *g*, we go up to the top and loop, down to the line, then down below it, and loop up again.")

Interventions for Creative Writing

The student with ADD often needs topic ideas or a summary before getting started on a writing task. Teach the student brainstorming techniques to help motivate the initial writing process. In brainstorming, you want to (1) provide a background of experiences and associations, (2) generate new ideas, and (3) aid in structure. Have students work in groups to write their ideas on sticky memo pads such as Post-it Notes. These are colorful and can be a fun way to get ideas started.

A brainstorming technique that employs mnemonic cuing is the 3 O's described by Salend (1990). The 3 O's stand for *Observing, Observing, Observing* and represent three separate ways to brainstorm ideas for a writing activity.

Observing #1. Look at a picture. List the details you see. Now propose sentences about them. Listing just the details helps you see how a paragraph can get started.

Observing #2. Pull together five different objects. Look at them. Compare their similarities. Write down how they are the same. Now write your paragraph.

Observing #3. Participate in an event (school assembly, movie, sports activity, and so on). Write descriptive words about what you saw. Organize the list and write a description of the event.

Spelling

Interestingly, parents of students with ADD often report that their children are able to get 100 percent on a spelling test. They practice the words briefly and can walk into a test and pass it with flying colors. *But* ask them the same words three days later—or have them write the words in a story—and they will misspell them.

The errors they make in spelling are characteristically errors of detail. They may leave out one letter of a word and misspell that word over and over again—sometimes in the same paragraph. These are examples of common spelling errors:

girl	gril
they	thuy
brother	bother
comb	combe
front	street

When you observe their spelling, you will see the word looks nearly correct, but one letter is missing or transposed. Here are some samples.

Sample #1

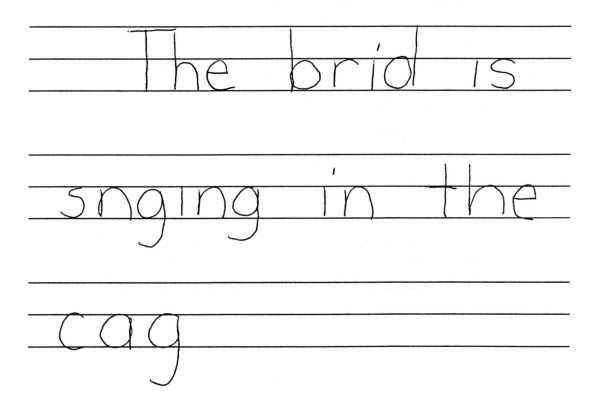

Sample #2

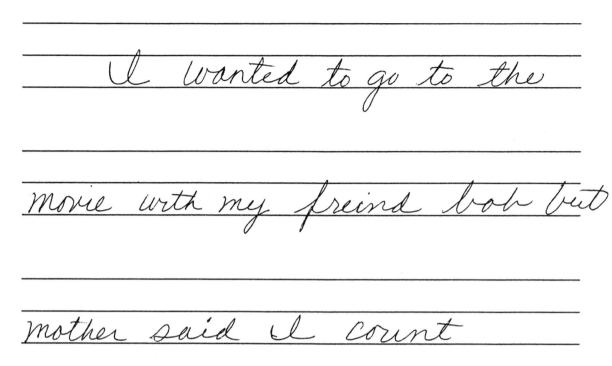

I wanted to go to the

movie with my freind bob but

mother said I count

Consider the following strategies to enhance spelling:

1. Use color cues on word flash cards to identify patterns within spelling words.

2. Teach the student to clap out the syllables while spelling.

3. Use manipulative letter sets to enhance recall and add a motor component to the task.

4. Teach students mnemonics for remembering word patterns, such as the following:

   • Do you see the "end" in friend?

   • Your school princi*pal* is your pal. A princi*ple* is a point.

   • I before E except after C.

5. Use the computer for spelling review. Its highly visual format makes it appealing for practice and rehearsal.

6. Allow students to take spelling tests orally or to audiotape them.

7. Consider assigning two grades to written projects: one for content and one for spelling. This way if the student's paper is creative and interesting, you can acknowledge this and avoid overpenalizing the student for spelling difficulty.

Figure 24

Tips for Coping with ADD/ADHD in the Classroom

If the student fidgets . . .

- Allow the student to finger one object. Encourage the student to hold a small Koosh ball or rubber ball, pipe cleaner, or sandpaper square.

- Redirect the student. Hand the child an object or book, redirecting the movement to a constructive task.

- For students who are continually tapping a pencil on the desk, model tapping on an arm or shoulder—and smile. Now you have quiet tapping.

- Ignore it!

If the student daydreams . . .

- Provide physical tasks and activities that require active participation. Example: giving "thumbs up" or "thumbs down" responses during a question-and-answer session.

- Encourage note-taking using mapping or webbing formats.

- Allow the student to doodle on a pad while listening to instructions.

- When confronted with a worksheet, suggest that the student use a colored pencil or highlighting marker to underline or emphasize directions.

- Reduce activities that require sustained attention. Allow the student structured opportunities to get up and move by going to get a drink or moving to a different seat.

- Place the student closer to you.

- Build variety into tasks and build success into the activity.

- Use peer tutors or allow the student to work with partners.

If the student calls out . . .

- Reward the student immediately when you observe him or her waiting to respond.

- Reinforce peers who do not call out.

- Provide cooperative learning experiences in which the student has more opportunities to share.

- Give every student three squares of paper. During a whole-class activity, if anyone calls out, remove a square from that student. Any students who have squares left at the end of the activity are rewarded with a predetermined privilege.

- Provide opportunities for the student to be involved in a leadership role with younger students.

Tips for Coping with ADD/ADHD in the Classroom
(continued)

If the student has difficulty working independently . . .

- Provide activities that have a sequential pattern and are within the child's range of ability.

- Write directions on a cue card and have student check off each direction as it is accomplished. Provide incentives for completing tasks.

- Present independent work as a sequential task in steps. Suggest that the student do step 1, then take a brief break at his or her desk before going on to step 2.

- Set a timer and tell the student, "I'll be back when this rings. See how many problems you can do before the buzzer goes off."

If the student has difficulty remembering . . .

- Use mnemonic strategies to cue recall.

- Encourage the student to verbally review information.

- Color code significant details.

- Teach the student visualization techniques.

- Have the student audiotape material and play back the tape for review.

74

Activities for Elementary Grades

There are certain times in the day when work is finished and the class is waiting to leave for another classroom or activity. They are waiting for the word to go, but there is a delay. This is a challenging time for kids with ADD, who begin to get restless and may bother others while waiting. These are activities to fill that time.

Goals   1. To employ a structured activity during a waiting period
              2. To build on the need for variety and high interest

Materials   Chalkboard

Instructions

Draw the outline of an automobile quickly on the board. Randomly print grade-level vocabulary words all over it. Each student finds a word, pronounces it, and then erases it. The object is to "wash the car" clean before the class must leave.

Variations

- Cover the car with basic math facts and use it as a math review.

- Write the names of state capitals, and have students name the corresponding state before they erase each word.

- Write the alphabet on the car. Students must come up in alphabetical order and erase one letter from their first names.

Goals   1. To employ a structured activity during a waiting period
2. To build on the need for variety and high interest

Materials   Index cards
Small colorful cloth drawstring bags
Your imagination

Instructions

Make several card games that can be stored in cloth bags. Place the bags by the door. When you have to wait with your class either by the door or in the hall, take a game out of the sack and offer an activity while waiting.

On each set of cards, you can make up a quick word game that involves the entire class. Example: pass out cards with state names on them. The student at the end of the line reads his or her card and passes it to the student in front, who must read both cards and pass them on. The students must read all the cards passed to them.

Other games: Write names of local restaurants on the cards. Students must read the name and say what they would order if they were there.

Write names of famous people: Each student must identify why that person is famous.

Variations

Put numbers on the cards. Have students draw one card apiece and line up numerically. Orally ask students to name their favorite cars, songs, sports, and so on, while you wait.

Memory Tricks: Remembering Homework Assignments

Students with attention deficits often forget to turn in assignments and homework. The following are a collection of ways to cue students that work is to be turned in.

Goals
1. To remember to return homework
2. To employ memory strategies

Materials
Colored paper
Markers
Paper dots
Colored envelopes
Erasable white board

Instructions

- Make a "homework" flag out of bright paper. Mount the flag by the door where students see it as they exit.

- Associate one color with each subject (example: red is for math). Then place a red paper dot on the chalkboard next to the math homework assignment. Next assign a nightly Homework Helper. At the end of the class, the Homework Helper gives students red dots to place on their own daily calendars.

- Provide students with a "phone tree" containing phone numbers of fellow classmates they can call to find out what their homework assignments are.

- Hand out homework assignments in brightly colored envelopes.

- Put a white board in the hall outside your room or in the window facing outside. Write homework assignments on the board.

Variations

Have the class sing the following song about homework. Audiotape it. As the class is gathering materials, coats, and homework at the end of the day, play the tape as a reminder.

Sung to the tune of "You Are My Sunshine":
I have _____ (math, science) homework
I have _____ homework; I have _____ homework.
I have _____ homework, I must do.
When I get home dear, then I must do it.
And bring it to school the next day.

Goals   1. To avoid students impulsively selecting a book that is too difficult
2. To help develop independent reading skills

Materials   Books

Instructions

This device has been around for years. It is appealing for the students with ADD because they respond to "catchy" tricks for remembering.

1. Have each student pick a book to read.

2. The student opens the book to the middle.

3. Ask the student to read silently.

4. When coming to an unfamiliar word, the student should put a finger on it.

5. If another unfamiliar word comes along, the student puts a finger on it, too.

6. If the student uses up all his or her fingers on one page, it might be a good idea to try another book!

Variations

Have students make a slash on a piece of scratch paper for every word they do not know. Four slashes = try another book!

Goals　　　　1. To reduce reading aloud during "silent" reading time
　　　　　　　　2. To help develop independent reading skills

Materials　　Books

Instructions

Students with ADD often do their "silent" reading out loud. Help them find a place where they can do so without bothering others and without feeling embarrassed about it. Don't make a big deal of their reading aloud. Remember, this is just one way that helps them concentrate.

Variations

- Allow the student to hold a pencil between the teeth when reading.

- If permitted by the school, gum chewing discourages the noisy reader.

- Play soft classical or piano music during silent reading time. This will often focus students and help them "tune out" other distractions, thereby reducing their need to "talk" through the task.

Listening Activity: Stop and Go

Goals
1. To encourage listening skills
2. To reduce impulsivity

Materials

Make a checkerboard pattern on a sheet of paper and photocopy it. Randomly color the squares red and green. Color the last square (in the bottom right-hand corner) black. Give each student a marker (or cubes, golf tees, poker chips, or other small manipulatives).

Instructions

Each student takes a turn as leader. The leader must make noise in some way that doesn't involve words or vocalization (examples are bouncing a ball, snapping fingers, tapping a foot). The students count how many times the leader makes the noise and move that number of spaces on the checkerboard. Students who land on a red square must move back one space. Students who land on a green square stay put. The first student to reach the black square wins.

Variations

The game continues until everyone in class has had a chance to be the leader. (When students reach the black square, they start over at the beginning.) When everyone has taken a turn as leader, students count to see how many times they reached the black square.

Goals   1. To improve turn-taking skills
             2. To reduce impulsive behavior

Materials
Take a standard deck of 52 cards and write a student's name on each card.

Instructions
When you are asking questions in a whole-class teaching exercise, use the card deck to select students to answer. Select a card at random and call on that student. Then set aside that card. This is very helpful in managing the class when many students know the answers and are vying for your attention.

Variations
Place students' names on tongue depressors or wooden craft sticks. Keep the sticks in a coffee can on your desk. As you call on a student, remove the corresponding stick and place it in a second can.

Goals	1. To increase memory for spelling words
	2. To build on visual strengths
Materials	Variety of colored pens and markers
	Colored index cards

Instructions

Put spelling words on index cards of different colors. Attempt wherever possible to group similar words on the same color card (for example, all nouns on blue cards, verbs on yellow). Or put words that have the same first letter or the same word ending on the same color card.

Variations

Use colored marking pens to mark prefixes, roots, and suffixes on each card. This helps alert students to spelling patterns.

Visual Spelling Techniques: Scrabble Letters

Goals   1. To increase memory for spelling words
2. To build on visual strengths

Materials   Box of letter tiles from a Scrabble word game set
Weekly spelling list

Instructions

Have the student take the weekly spelling list and divide it into groups of three. If there is anything similar about the sets of three words or if they can be divided by categories, this will aid recall. Then have the student spell out each word using the letter tiles. When the student is actively involved in moving the letters, there is more interest in studying the words.

Variations

Have the student spell out the words with the letter tiles, then type the words from the tiles on the computer. Magnetic letters placed on a metal board or the side of a filing cabinet can be used in the same way.

84

Goals	1. To increase memory for spelling words
	2. To build on visual strengths

Materials	Squares of black construction paper about photo size (3" x 5")
	White chalk

Instructions

Tell the students to imagine that their eyes are a camera. When they look at a word they are trying to memorize, they should "take a picture" of it with their eyes. Hand them each a square of black construction paper and a piece of white chalk. Tell them to "develop" their pictures by writing the word on the paper. Next they should compare their "picture" with the original word. The process is repeated until they can "take a good picture" (spell the word right).

Variations

Visualization skills can also be developed without the written component. Students should be encouraged to visualize the word and then spell it aloud.

Goals	1. To increase attention to spelling tasks
	2. To develop sequencing skills
Materials	Index cards
	Clear acetate
	Marker

Instructions

When a student consistently misspells the same word, place the word on a regular index card; on a piece of clear acetate print another word with which it is commonly confused or write the word the way the student misspells it. Place the acetate on top of the card. Have the student note where the two words differ.

Variations

Have students write the word correctly using a variety of media: large marking pens, multicolored pens, chalk, on a computer. Have the student write on different materials: sandpaper, brown paper bags, white boards, colored lined paper.

Copyright © 1994 by Communication Skill Builders, a division of The Psychological Corporation / All rights reserved / 1-800-228-0752 / ISBN 07616671951

Visual Spelling Techniques: Configuration Clues

Goals   1. To increase attention to spelling tasks
                 2. To help students use their visual gestalt skills

Materials   Different lengths of heavy card stock
                 Colored markers

Instructions

Use visual tricks to help students remember words and letters that are commonly confused. Example: If the child confuses the letters "b" and "d," take the word "bed" and have the student trace around the word, making the drawing look like an actual bed.

Variations

Have students write words using cartoons or simple drawings to illustrate the word's meaning.

Goals	1. To employ variety and brevity in a spelling test
	2. To build on visual strengths

Materials   Set of alphabet cards or alphabet letter tiles for each student
Poker chips, cubes, or toothpicks (one chip per student for each word on the spelling test)

Instructions

Have students pair up. Read the weekly spelling test to students. Each student uses the alphabet tiles or cards to spell out the word. The partners check each other's words against your model. Each student receives one chip for each correct word.

Variations

Make a chart assigning a grade to each number of chips. For example: On a 10-word spelling test, 10 chips = A.

Goals
1. To improve sequencing skills
2. To build on students' need for variety and high interest
3. To incorporate physical activity in a task

Materials
Strips of tagboard or manila folders cut to 3" x 12"
Colored construction paper cut into 2" x 2" squares
Stapler
Marker

Instructions

Write one basal vocabulary word on each side of five construction paper squares (write the words near the tops of the cards). Include a variety of nouns, verbs, and articles. Fold the manila strips lengthwise so that 1 inch of the 3-inch side is turned up. Staple at each end to make a holder for the cards. Give each student a sentence holder and five word cards (representing different word classes). Have the student make up as many sentences as possible, always using all five cards.

Variations

Write dates, events, steps in a process, directions for making an art project, or similar sequential information on sets of cards. Have the child arrange each set of cards in sequential order (chronologically or logically).

Goals
1. To encourage sequencing skills
2. To develop skills for responding to detailed questions regarding content material

Materials

Draw a jet airplane on a large sheet of construction paper. Divide the plane into three separate sections. Label the first section with the number 1 and the word "What," the second section with 2 and "Where?" and the third with 3 and "When?"

Cut out word cards shaped as seats. On each card, write a word that can be used to answer a "what," "where," or "when" question.

Instructions

The student selects three word cards and reads them, then places each word in the section of the plane corresponding to the information it provides.

Variations

Draw the plane on the front of a manila folder and staple a pocket inside to hold the seat cards. The game can easily be stored in a file cabinet or learning center. It can also be played with the entire class by drawing an airplane on an overhead transparency.

Cartoon Character Board

Goals
1. To identify beginning, middle, and ending consonant sounds
2. To build on students' need for variety and high interest
3. To employ physical activity in a task

Materials
Green file folders
Drawing of cartoon character
Tongue depressors
List of words containing specific consonant sounds

Instructions
This lesson reinforces listening for consonant sounds.

Duplicate the drawing of a popular cartoon character on the front of each green file folder (make one folder for every class member). Place a tongue depressor inside each file folder.

Tell the students a particular letter sound that they should listen for. Read a word from your list. The students use the tongue depressor to tap the head of the cartoon character if the letter sound is heard at the beginning of the word. If the sound is in the middle, they tap the character's stomach, and if it's at the end, they tap the character's feet.

Variations
Laminate the folders and substitute a grease pencil or felt-tip marker for the tongue depressor. Students make a mark on the character to indicate the location of the letter sound, then wipe off the mark before the next word is presented.

Goals	1. To learn word families
	2. To build on students' need for variety and high interest
	3. To incorporate physical activity into a task

Materials	Brown construction paper (11" x 18")
	White circles (about the size of a baseball)
	Pronged paper fasteners (brads)

Instructions

Cut the brown construction paper into 16 catcher's mitts the size of a student's hand. Staple pairs of mitt shapes together so they make a glove that will fit over the student's hand. Write words from a single word family in a circle around the outside of each "baseball" (white circle). Attach a ball to each mitt with a brad. Have students team with a partner. Each pair of students is given a mitt. One student wears the mitt and must turn the ball in the center around while the partner says the words printed on the ball. The partner then takes a turn wearing the mitt.

Examples

Here are sample word families that could be used on the mitts:

Mitt #1: __all

Mitt #2: __an

Mitt #3: __ain

Mitt #4: __ay

Mitt #5: __y

Mitt #6: __ight

Mitt #7: __ook

Mitt #8: __ill

Goals   1. To provide strategies for remembering phonics rules
2. To use students' visual and movement strengths

Materials   None required

Instructions

Incorporate students' need for movement and their recall skills for the unique by using body cues to help them recall sound-symbol relationships. After the use of associative cues has been modeled by the instructor, students can generate their own associations. Associate a sound, blend, or vowel cluster with a physical cue. For example: "Ch" can be taught by saying, "It's like a train, ch . . . ch . . . ch." Or "Sh" can be shown by placing an index finger to your lips and pantomiming "shhh" for quiet.

Variations

The Open Court reading series and The Spaulding Technique incorporate this type of cuing in their reading instruction.

Goals   1. To provide strategies for remembering phonics rules
              2. To help develop visual gestalt strengths

Materials   Paper
              Colored pens
              Notebook rings
              Hole punch

Instructions

Introduce groups of words that contain a common word pattern. (Examples: words ending in ___it, ___tion, ___ay, ___ight). Write the words on flash cards. Emphasize visual similarities by writing the letters that are identical in the words in a specific color. Punch a hole in each word card. Put all words from one family on the same notebook ring. Students can keep the rings in their desks for practice and review.

Variations

For additional practice, take the cards off the rings and arrange them with identical parts aligned vertically. Example:

m *ight*

fl *ight*

t *ight*

*From Telzrow and Speer (1986)

94

Goals
1. To employ physical activity during a lesson
2. To build on students' need for variety and high interest
3. To improve identification of vowel sounds

Materials
40 round cards with vowels on them
Tagboard
Markers

Instructions

Make up eight game cards from tagboard (see diagram below), each card containing five three- or four-letter words. In place of the vowel in each word, draw a circle the size of the vowel cards. Next to each word, write its definition. Each student is given a game card. Place the vowel circle cards face down in a pile on the table. Each student in turn draws a vowel circle card and may use that circle on the game card if it will fit in any of the blank circles to make a word that corresponds with the definition. If not, the vowel circle is put in a discard pile. Each child who places a circle on the game card should read the resulting word and the definition beside it.

Examples

R ( ) G = We walk on it.

S ( ) D = We are not happy.

P ( ) T = A boy's or a girl's name.

L ( ) D = The top of a pan.

B ( ) D = We sleep on it.

Goals	1. To increase recall for long vowel sounds
	2. To develop skills for working cooperatively in groups

Materials	Paper
	Pencils
	Overhead projector
	Words written on a transparency

Instructions

This game is best played with groups of students. Each student needs a paper with five houses drawn on it near the top of the page. Each house is labeled with a vowel. Place a list of words from the current class reading series on the overhead projector. The object of the game is to write the words on the overhead under the correct house. The teacher reads five words, then the students write those words in the correct locations. The team that writes the words under the correct houses wins.

Variations

This game can also be used with one or two students. In this case, write the list on a piece of paper rather than a transparency.

Goals
1. To increase recognition of contractions
2. To develop skills for working cooperatively in a group

Materials
Paper
Chalkboard or erasable board

Instructions

Children with ADD, who pass over little details, consider contractions boring stuff. Make practice more enjoyable by using a game format to encourage learning. Make a tic-tac-toe grid on the board and write a contraction in each box. The game is played just like regular tic-tac-toe. However, before placing an X or an O in a box, the player must read the contraction out loud, say the two words which make up the contraction, and use the contraction in a sentence.

Goals
1. To increase ability to notice details in words
2. To develop skills for working cooperatively in a group

Materials
Paper
Chalkboard or erasable board

Instructions

Have students work in pairs. Each partner chooses a word for the other. You specify the number of letters all the words must have. The words are written with only the first and last letters and a blank between them, as shown in these examples:

O_____R

N_____D

R_____G

When each student has drawn the first and last letters of a word, the partner tries to fill in the blank with letters to complete the word. Students score one point for every correct letter. The person with the highest number of points wins.

Variations

Put the game on the overhead projector and have the entire class guess the words. This is a great way to review before a unit or chapter spelling test.

Goals   1. To employ physical activity during a lesson
2. To build on students' need for variety and high interest

Materials   A hopscotch pattern marked on the floor with tape
Beanbags
Picture cards
Vowel cards

Instructions

Place a picture card in the corner of each square of the hopscotch board. The student tosses a beanbag and hops to the square where it landed. The child picks up the picture and must identify the initial sound in that word and the letter that makes the sound. Replace the cards as they are picked up.

Next show a vowel card and say the vowel sound. The student must hop to a square containing a picture of a word that has the vowel sound in it.

Variations

Add some auditory and listening practice. Tell the child how many squares to hop on the hopscotch grid and whether to pick up the card on the way down or the way back. Gradually add two directions: "Pick up a card with an 'r' sound on your way down and one with an 'm' sound on your way back."

Goals
1. To employ physical activity during a lesson
2. To build on students' need for variety and high interest

Materials
Pretzel sticks (long sticks about 8" long and short sticks 2" long)
Rulers
Overhead projector or chalkboard

Instructions

Take out one stick. Hold it in front of students and ask, "How many inches long do you think this stick is?" Have them write down their estimates. Pass out pretzels. Have students measure their pretzels with a ruler and write down the actual length. Then students bite a piece off one end of their pretzels. They estimate the new length of the pretzel, record that number, then measure the actual length and record it. Ask students to give you the actual lengths they measured after taking a bite from the pretzel. Write all the lengths down and show the class how to average them. Repeat the exercise with a small pretzel.

Variations

Fill a large jar with peanuts in the shell or marshmallows. Have students submit estimates on the number of goodies they think are in the jar. The three students making the closest estimates get to divide the contents of the jar.

Goals   1. To increase memory for fraction rules
                            2. To develop visual gestalt strengths

Materials   Index cards
                         Hole punch
                         Notebook rings

Instructions

Present a division problem (or any other multistep problem) in a flip-chart format. Make up a model problem, writing each step on a separate card. Place the cards in order on a notebook ring so the student can quickly flip back and forth between the steps.

Example

Identify the divisor.

$$\frac{1}{2} \div \frac{3}{4}$$

Invert the divisor.

$$\frac{3}{4} \text{ becomes } \frac{4}{3}$$

Multiply the fractions and reduce to the lowest terms.

$$\frac{1}{2} \times \frac{4}{3} = \frac{4}{6} = \frac{2}{3}$$

Variations

Have each index card be a different color. Have the student color code each step to match the corresponding index card while completing the problem.

Goals
1. To improve memory for a multistep problem
2. To develop visual gestalt strengths

Materials
Paper
Chalkboard or erasable board

Instructions

When teaching a long division model, use mnemonic codes to help the student remember each step. For example, assume the steps are: Divide, Multiply, Subtract, Bring down, Repeat steps, Check. State the following to students: "We need a family to do this problem."

D(ivide)	=	Dad
M(ultiply)	=	Mom
S(ubtract)	=	Sister
B(ring down)	=	Brother
R(epeat steps)	=	Relatives
C(heck)	=	Cousins

Variations

Make a visual model to aid recall for the steps in the problem.

Goals   1. To increase attention to reading tasks
                      2. To develop independent reading skills

Materials   Different lengths of heavy card stock
                      Scissors
                      File folders

Instructions

Many students with ADD have difficulty following the printed line as they read. Provide a variety of different bookmarks to encourage their attention to the word in front of them.

- An L shape cut out of card stock can help students focus on words and locate answers on multiple-choice tests. Students line up the horizontal leg of the L on a row of text.

- In a piece of card stock, cut an opening that is just large enough to expose about three words at a time. Have the student move this card along the row of print while reading.

Variations

To help increase attention to math problems, try this variation. Use a manila file folder to help with math worksheets. Cut out several distinct shapes on the cover of the folder. Place the file folder over the worksheet and tell the student to work on just the problems showing through the holes. Tell the student you will be back when the task is completed. When you return, remove the sheet and have the student finish the problems that have not been completed.

Chapter 5
What Works? Approaches for the Middle School and High School Years

I can't bear to think of middle school. My son will never function. He can't remember his backpack; how will he remember six different teachers?
—Mother of a 12-year-old boy

You should know better by now! You learned this in fifth grade.
—Teacher in a freshman math class

Middle school? . . . *Boring* with a capital B!
—14-year-old boy with ADD

Watch my lips, I'm only going to say this once. I should not have to repeat to a class of sophomores!
—Teacher in a high school English class

By adolescence, many professionals hope that the symptoms of attention disorders will diminish in intensity. In fact, for years some physicians have recommended that children cease taking medication for ADD during puberty. It was felt that children would outgrow their attention problems by about that time. A review of the related research regarding adolescent behavior, however, indicates that young adults continue to experience significant problems with ADD (Milich and Loney 1979). About 25 percent of adolescents with ADD have problems with antisocial behavior such as fighting, occasional moderate marijuana use, and minor delinquency. Many also have failed a grade by this time, and overall their achievement is low compared to that of their classmates (Friedman and Doyal 1992). Four-fifths are behind by one or more years in at least one basic academic subject (Loney, Kramer, and Milich 1981).

Human beings are a goal-directed species. Inherent in our behavior is the desire to satisfy our needs and wants in order to attain a level of happiness equal to our ideals. The goal of an adolescent is often to achieve a sense of identity while avoiding inferiority. Parental influence begins to decline, and there is more independent responsibility for schoolwork, household chores, and sexual conduct. For adolescents with ADD, these increased responsibilities are in serious conflict with their delays in developing judgment, persistence, self-awareness, and goal-directed behavior (Barkley 1990). According to Barkley, as many as 75 percent of adolescents with ADD will continue to evidence problems in school, home, or community adjustment.

The essential characteristics of the disorder—inattention, impulsivity, and hyperactivity—continue, but in varying degrees for each adolescent. One teenager may now sit in his seat in the classroom for an entire day but exhibit his impulsivity behind the wheel of a car. Another child entering into adolescence may conquer her organizational weaknesses only to find her temper and poor coping skills hinder her from social success in high school.

Self-Esteem

Self-esteem is a critical psychological need and an important concept to understand. In *Webster's Dictionary,* it is defined as "one's good opinion of one's self." To esteem something or someone means to highly value the thing or person. For the normal adolescent, self-esteem is shaky at best—moving quickly from levels of egocentricity to self-loathing. For youngsters with ADD, self-esteem tends to plummet because they are expected to have greater self-control and have more internal responsibility than they can exhibit. The educational environment into which they have now entered expects them to negotiate with six different teachers, remember six different room locations, and follow six separate class syllabi—not to mention remembering a student identification number and locker combination! The American educational system is designed with the best interests of the adolescent with ADHD at the bottom of the list (Goldstein and Goldstein 1990). Students with ADD struggle to keep up, but they begin to feel more overwhelmed and inadequate. As one of Paul Wender's patients observed, when life is characterized by "no hits, no runs, and plenty of errors, you do not have a terrific view of yourself" (Wender 1987).

Depression

Research has indicated that a significant proportion of inattentive adolescents present with symptoms of depression (Cantwell 1979). Adolescent depression is a subtle and dangerous phenomenon. The alert adult may notice increased symptoms of depression and some skill regression during the onset of puberty at the beginning of middle school. Professionals must be very aware of students' silent cries for help. Adolescents are masters at hiding their emotions. They can appear just fine even when they are struggling to keep it together.

Noncompliance and Incompetence

As the subject matter and responsibilities increase, the student with ADD can begin to slip behind, and by the end of the grading period, be lost and failing! Without intervention, such an adolescent may begin to regress and could develop characteristics of opposition defiance disorder (ODD) or conduct disorder (CD).

For some educators, identifying when a behavior results from an attention disorder and when it is noncompliance can be challenging. It is difficult to separate the behaviors typical of teenagers from those that are a result of this frustrating disorder. For example, poor planning skills can easily be mistaken for indifference to school or teachers' requests. Incompetence for the adolescent with ADD will be demonstrated through difficulties with attention, memory, and impulsivity. When we observe these behaviors, we must respond with honest communication, modeling, and skill-building. On the other hand, noncompliance—where the student flat-out refuses a request and is belligerent, rude, or threatening about it—should be met with withdrawal of privileges and punishment. By successfully distinguishing between incompetent and noncompliant behavior, parents and professionals can reduce negative feedback, increase compliance and success, and stem the tide of development of oppositional behavioral patterns (Goldstein and Goldstein 1990).

Gifted Adolescents with ADD/ADHD

The adolescent with ADD whose ability falls in the gifted or very superior range—IQ of 130 or higher—is often a major challenge for educators. It is difficult to set reasonable expectations for these students. They appear to be highly intelligent, intensely curious, and quick-witted. Because they have actually learned the academic material, they have high expectations for themselves. Therefore, when they are met with repeated disappointments in their performance, they often react by projecting an "I don't care" image.

These frustrations and disappointments are all caused by misunderstanding of the nature of giftedness and ADHD (Murphy 1989). Giftedness represents primarily the potential to learn. ADD, on the other hand, is a productivity handicap which affects grades. Because school performance is measured through grades, good performance requires the very attributes that many adolescents with ADD lack. When the adults in this child's life do not reconcile the conflict between potential and performance, they mistake incompetence for noncompliance (Mashburn 1991). The non-performing gifted child is continually reminded of his or her failure to perform up to expectations. This reaction from well-meaning but ignorant professionals can lead the adolescent to serious behavior disorders.

Putting on the Brakes

Every educator who cares about children wants to make a difference in their lives. As we view the world of the adolescent with ADD, we must ask how we can halt this downward spiral. How can we help this child feel valued and productive?

One answer lies in the research of Weiss and Hechtman (1986). This longitudinal study followed a group of 75 children diagnosed with ADHD into adulthood. The participants were interviewed about the influence growing up with ADD had on their lives and what areas they, as adults, wanted to change. They were asked what had helped them the most through their lives. Most responded that one person had believed in them, someone ranging from a parent to a teacher to a friend. They described this significant person as inspirational and directional. In addition, the majority had not liked taking medication, nor did they feel they had been given enough information about the medication or how it worked.

Studies of this type have significant implications for helping us identify interventions that might have been introduced earlier in these people's lives and might have resulted in a more successful path. If we can impress upon adolescents the nature of their strengths, perhaps we can guide them to use these strengths in coping with their weaknesses. The quest for professionals is to develop in every adolescent with ADD a cadre of resiliency factors—buffers if you will—that they can draw on. As educational professionals, we need to direct our energies to help adolescents recognize that they do have strengths and what these strengths are. If we can counsel adolescents into understanding their value and potential, we can effect a better prognosis for the future.

Developing Resiliency

The following are suggestions that professionals in secondary schools can apply to develop resiliency skills in adolescents with ADD:

1. Adolescents, especially those with ADD, need one person in their lives who relates to them with unconditional acceptance. This person can be a teacher, a parent, a friend, or anyone as long as the teen perceives that this person accepts him or her no matter what.

2. The adolescent will need guidance and role-modeling to develop stronger interpersonal relationships. Many times, the impulsivity and intense emotions typical of ADD hinder the teen in developing relationships with peers. Yet the child with ADD has a natural sensitivity to others that goes unnoticed. This sensitivity needs to be reinforced. Provide the student with a mentor within the academic situation. It is helpful for the student to have one adult who serves as a personal advisor on an informal basis.

3. Accept that students with ADD may resist formal classes because of their highly predictable format. Present opportunities for these students to develop creative and artistic talents within the class. Help them explore and invent. For example, allow the student to audiotape rather than write a book review or to present a poster in lieu of a report.

4. Reinforce and nurture the student's natural gestalt or global skills by offering videos, experiences of travel, trips to museums, and visits to the theater.

5. Encourage the adolescent to develop a lifelong habit of journal/diary writing, poetry writing, or audiotaping personal recollections. Suggest that students use these tools to vent and clarify their feelings.

Cognitive restructuring may also be needed to help these adolescents alter their belief systems. It is important to identify inappropriate cognition, provide a logical challenge to it, and suggest alternative, healthier thought patterns (Barkley 1990). Barkley suggests that the adolescent, with the help of a therapist, design an experiment to disprove an unreasonable cognition. Barkley gave the example of a young man who complained that his parents were always asking him to do chores around the yard. Barkley asked this student to record in a journal every time his parents asked him to do extra work. After several weeks of documentation, the journal was examined. The teen was surprised to find that he had been asked fewer than five times. He had really believed until he documented the information that his parents were constantly badgering him. This journal writing activity failed to support his unreasonable cognition.

Creating a Positive School Environment

Here is a list of strategies to foster a healthy school environment for students with ADD.

1. Allow educational accommodations to be made. When you make accommodations, you are tailoring your teaching style to meet the student's needs.

2. Provide times in your class for organizational interventions: writing down homework assignments, reviewing before a test, collecting materials, storing materials.

3. Avoid sarcasm. The adolescent with ADD hears negative comments from people 80 percent of the time. Don't add to it. Express your expectations clearly to avoid a need for sarcastic retort. Treat the student with dignity, remembering that in doing so, you are modeling social skills for the student.

4. Set up creative opportunities for one-on-one instruction (peer tutoring, volunteer aides) and small-group instruction. Avoid lengthy lectures to the whole class.

5. Design your classes for brevity and variety.

6. Employ visuals to encourage inattentive learners and enhance their interest.

7. Break down tasks into smaller steps; present directions in steps.

8. Make tasks meaningful for students and relevant to their interests.

9. Offer a variety of testing measures. Incorporate a selection of testing implements to help capture the students' different strengths.

10. Schedule time for periodic one-on-one meetings with the student to see how things are going. Offer the use of a peer counselor.

Questioning Techniques

Teenagers with ADD need to be active participants in the classroom to stay alert and to be able to interact within the educational environment. They will need to ask questions to clarify information they may have missed during a verbal presentation. When checking for comprehension, ask questions that have all students respond in a direct manner. Mastropieri and Scruggs (1991) recommend the following questioning strategies:

1. Avoid targeting a single student by name with a question. Instead, start your questions with phrases such as, "Everyone listen, here is my question . . ." or, "I want you all to think before you answer. . . ."

2. Randomly select students to respond to questions and allow them at least ten seconds to formulate an answer. Teachers in the United States usually answer their own questions if no one has responded within about half a second. By waiting a few seconds to give students time to formulate their responses, you are likely to get better and more complete answers.

3. Use choral questioning, in which students respond in unison on a cue from you. For example: "Everyone in Shakena's group say the answer."

4. When many students attempt to reply to a question and you are not sure whom to choose, rely on a deck of name cards. Select one card at random and ask the student whose name you drew to reply.

5. Let students respond to yes/no questions by giving a "thumbs up" or "thumbs down" sign or by holding up a card marked "yes" or "no."

Whole-Class Listening Activity

Research indicates that teachers give more than 200 instructional statements each day (Lovitt and Smith 1972). Listening—attending aurally and responding correctly—in a group situation is very challenging for students with ADD. Yet these skills are an important part of school success, and students are expected to display them throughout their day.

The LISTEN strategy program is based on an acronym that functions as a mnemonic device to help the student with ADD acquire and improve listening skills in a whole-class listening activity. This strategy, created by Jeanne Bauwens and Jack J. Hourcode (1989), can help to increase students' overall attention span and decrease the number of times the teacher has to repeat information. It can also increase the frequency and quality of positive interactions between teacher and student.

In trials of the strategy, the teacher instructed the student to listen and then said:

1. **L** ook.
2. **I** dle your motor.
3. **S** it up straight.
4. **T** urn to me.
5. **E** ngage your brain.
6. **N** ow . . .

Visual reinforcement was provided by listing the six LISTEN instructions on 3" x 5" cards on each student's desk, as well as on a large colorful poster in front of the room. Initially, the teacher paused after saying each step out loud, but gradually these pauses were eliminated as students became familiar with the procedure. Eventually the teacher faded the amount of assistance, merely pointing to the six steps and repeating each of the letters.

After several days, the teacher was able to simply say, "LISTEN," and the students reviewed the acronym silently. According to Bauwens and Hourcode (1989), all teachers testing the method reported consistent gains in class attention to oral group instructions.

Peer Tutoring

In peer tutoring, one student works with another student under the guidance of a teacher. This technique is well recognized by education professionals and is employed in schools everywhere. No one will dispute the benefits of this powerful peer-driven strategy.

Because of their need for one-on-one instruction, students with ADD will definitely benefit from such a technique. It has been my experience, however, that they rarely get to participate in peer situations because adults fear they will be unable to control their behavior with another student. We need to develop interventions that allow students with ADD to benefit from individual one-on-one time.

Suggestions for peer tutoring

1. Match the student with a strong peer model whenever possible. Role model expected behaviors for the partners.

2. Place a laminated cue card on the table where tutoring will take place. List each step or goal you expect to be accomplished. Designate one member of the team to be responsible for checking off each goal as it is accomplished.

3. Set a timer for the expected length of the session. This will help the student with ADD, who needs a visual way to monitor the beginning and end of the activity.

4. Periodically check in with the tutoring team to monitor how the pair are succeeding. Be alert so you can catch possible problems immediately.

5. Provide visual reinforcement by using a chart to mark tutoring time. Use verbal encouragement to help students feel positive about their involvement.

6. The student with attention disorders will also benefit greatly from the opportunity to tutor other students.

Visual Depictions

Strong visual modeling aids that support the curriculum will be very appealing to teens with ADD/ADHD. If you illustrate with drawings or symbols the information you are trying to convey, you will be more successful with inattentive students. Graphs, charts, symbols, rebus characters, arrows, boxes, and the like can all serve as strong visual support. These students' strong visual gestalt skills make any instruction employing visual depictions intrinsically interesting to them. Figure 25 illustrates three different ways to make the written word more visually appealing.

Figure 25
Visual Cues

The 3 physical states of water =

1. Liquid
2. Solid
3. Gas

Many people learn ☐best☐ from first-hand experiences—from working directly with other people and materials, building on what they already know.

Remember!

☐Your☐ sentence should include:

>>> C S P C E <<<

C: Capital Letter
S: Subject
P: Predicate
C: Complete Thought
E: End mark

Planning

The impulsive, inattentive student rarely makes plans or sets up steps for accomplishing a task. Therefore, we can help this student by providing step-by-step instructions, modeling planning skills, and employing visual strategies that cue the student to the stages of an activity. Think of this student as someone who does not acquire planning skills naturally but needs much direct instruction to develop them.

Figures 26 and 27 summarize instructional strategies that assist middle school and high school students. Figure 28 gives interventions for specific difficulties common to students with ADD.

Figure 26
Middle School: What Works?

Advance Organization
- Background information before new tasks
- An opportunity to tour school campus prior to the start of the school year and locate the actual rooms where classes will be held
- Practice opening padlocks

Daily Organization
- Order and routine in the classroom
- Schedules posted
- Color-coded materials
- A supply of extra pencils for teacher to hand out
- Designated places for materials

Study Skills
- Opportunities to learn study strategies such as SQ3R (see chapter 6)
- Tutors to help students organize and keep up with daily work

Attention
- Mnemonic strategies (see chapters 5 and 6)
- Strong visual depictions
- Lessons presented in short, brief segments
- Notes and visual cues put on overhead transparency during lectures
- Opportunities for controlled movement within the classroom
- Audiotapes of lessons

Planning Skills
- Variety and novelty in lessons; avoid rote
- Opportunities for small-group learning
- Peer tutoring

Figure 27
High School: What Works?

- Experience-based curriculum (prior associations enhance success)
- Use of demonstrations and role playing
- Cooperative learning groups
- Hands-on experiences and activities
- Project-oriented curriculum (accommodates a variety of learning styles and experiences)
- Multimedia technology: computer, videotapes, interactive video
- Mentorship/internship; coaching/tutoring
- Learning games and mind challenges
- Compensatory strategies: hand speller, calculator, study outlines, tape recorder, note-taking strategies
- Teacher selection: matching teacher's style to students' strengths.

Figure 28

Coping with the Middle School/High School Student Who Has ADD/ADHD

Challenge: The student has poor note-taking skills.

- Hand out a written format for note-taking before class, employ webbing and mapping formats.

- Allow student to audiotape the class.

- Provide a typed outline of discussion. Leave room for students to write in comments.

- Designate a "class note-taker" each day. After class, photocopy these notes and make them available to anyone who needs them.

- Put an outline of your lecture on a colored transparency and display it on the overhead. Put key words on the outline.

- Stop periodically and ask students to summarize what you have just said in their own words.

- Number or alphabetize any information you put on the board or overheads so students can follow along more easily.

- Allow students to use pastel-colored paper to add diversity and interest to their daily note-taking.

- Once a week, review notes with the class. Have them use highlighting markers to feature special areas in their notes.

- Periodically collect notes and analyze them to see how you can better help students to keep up in class.

Challenge: The student has poor organizational skills.

- Designate one homeroom as an organizational homeroom. The teacher in this homeroom has all the students' assignments for the day and assists students in recording them. Students return to the homeroom at the end of the day to ensure that they have everything they need to complete their homework.

- Allow students to keep one book in class and one book at home so they do not have to transport books.

- Use voice mail for homework assignments. Students can call the school for assignments.

- Send home a monthly schedule of tests and assignments. Leave a second set in the school office for parents to pick up.

- Assign study buddies to work together for the last five minutes of the period. Partners check to see whether homework has been handed in and the next assignment has been recorded.

- Have one well-marked place where students return papers. Have row captains check that everyone has handed in homework.

- Assign a study phone buddy to each student. This way, a student can call an assigned classmate to discuss homework, upcoming tests, and other questions.

Challenge: The student has difficulty copying written work from the board to paper or from a book to a workbook or paper.

- Add visual clues to information you write on the board.

- Number material students are to copy.

- Block off part of the visual material for the student, to help reduce distractions.

- Allow the student to use a clipboard when copying. The clipboard provides a smooth surface, and the student can sit in a variety of ways, yet still have a firm surface for writing.

- Highlight sections of a worksheet with color for easier recall.

- Place a colored transparency (red or yellow) over dulled photocopied worksheets to add crispness and clarity to the printed word.

- Reduce writing tasks. Allow the student alternative ways to demonstrate comprehension of the material; for example, by audiotaping a response.

Challenge: The student has difficulty concentrating when reading silently at a desk.

- Employ "read to the clip" technique described on page 123.

- Allow the student to place a colored note card on the page to mark the line being read and to cover some of the paragraphs from view.

- Have two students take turns reading aloud to each other at the back of the room.

- Allow the student to sit on the floor to read or to stand at the side of the room.

- Suggest that the student take a "daydream" break every five minutes. After reading for five minutes, the student can close the book and look away or "daydream" for one minute. Give the student a timer to use.

- Allow the student to listen to a book on audiotape before reading it to set up a visualization of the material—prior association often increases comprehension.

- Provide a one-paragraph summary of each chapter that student can review several days later to enhance recall.

- Allow students to jot down specific details on paper as they read.

Activities for
Middle School and
High School

Goals	1. To provide an activity that will help students leave an unstructured activity and move toward a more formal one 2. To improve self-management skills
Materials	Two minutes at beginning of class period Two minutes at conclusion of class period

Instructions

At the beginning of class, offer students two minutes to review with a fellow classmate information in their notes from the previous day's class. Sometimes assign students to teams; other times allow students to pick whomever they wish to work with.

This introductory review will direct students' immediate attention to the subject to be discussed and enhance their memory. The class will be more focused on the discussion, having just reviewed material.

At the end of class, again allow a few minutes for reviewing the material just learned. This can be a whole-class, team, or teacher-directed review. Put an outline of the material covered on the overhead projector and go over key points.

Variations

Assign two students daily to be class reporters. At the end of class, they are responsible for sharing what was discussed with the class. This strategy uses peer learning and is particularly successful with high school students.

Goals   1. To ease transitions
                     2. To improve self-management skills

Materials   Overhead projector
                 Paper

Instructions

Students with ADD have difficulty with transitions where they are leaving an unstructured time and entering a structured time. At the beginning of each class, provide a high-interest activity on the overhead projector to motivate students and capture their initial interest when entering the room. You can also write questions on the overhead for students to answer as they enter.

Variations

1. Put various contemporary advertising slogans on the overhead and see whether students can match them with the products they promote. Examples:

   - "You deserve a break today."

   - "Just do it!"

   - "Choosy mothers choose _____."

   - "Finger lickin' good!"

   - "Get a piece of the rock."

   - "Don't squeeze the _____."

   - "The ultimate Driving Machine."

   (**Answers:** McDonald's; Nike; Jif; Kentucky Fried Chicken; Prudential; Charmin; BMW)

2. Have students list their top five favorite movies, car models, performers, states, or whatever.

3. Ask questions relating to school events: Who was just elected class secretary? What was the score of the game last night? Keep the questions high-interest and age-appropriate.

Goals   1. To increase time on task during study hall
2. To improve self-management skills

Materials   Accountability sheet photocopied on colored paper

Instructions

Students with ADD have a difficult time during study hall because it is generally an unstructured activity for them. Provide a daily "accountability sheet" on which students must record what they do during the time.

Include a space on the accountability sheet for name and class period. Then type: "What did I accomplish in study hall today?" Make five large boxes under the question. Label the spaces with the days from Monday through Friday (or whatever days the study hall meets).

These students often need help to start using this sheet effectively; here's one way to help. Collect accountability sheets from several days and review how the student is using study hall time. Discuss with the student some practical time-management strategies.

Filling Time: "Give Me One Minute of Your Time!"

Goals
1. To provide an activity that will help students leave an unstructured activity and move to a more formal one
2. To improve self-management skills
3. To fill an unplanned time in the day

Materials   None

Instructions

There are certain times during the day when for various reasons you are left with just a few minutes of unplanned time on your hands. This is a difficult time for inattentive students because they are challenged by independent free time. This activity can fill that time in a productive way.

Tell the class, "Sometimes we wish people would give us just one minute of their time to share something with us—just one minute! Here's an activity where you will get your chance."

Divide the class into pairs (Count off 1—2, 1—2 . . .). Tell the students: "Number 1s, you will go first; you have one minute to tell your partner all the things you plan to do over vacation next week. Number 2s, you must just listen. No words. You can use facial expressions but no words."

Set a timer and start the activity immediately. When the timer rings, Number 1s and Number 2s switch off. Set the timer again.

Variations

You can vary the topic to incorporate whatever the class is currently studying. This activity can also be helpful when two students are not getting along. Take them aside and use this technique to get both sides of the story. Then give them another minute to come up with solutions for resolving the disagreement.

Goals   1. To reduce impulsivity
            2. To improve self-management skills

Materials   None

Instructions

Students with ADD often hand in papers they have finished very quickly with no attention to details or minor errors. The teacher usually responds, "I see some errors on this page. Look it over." The impulsive student often responds by glancing at the page again and stating, "I don't see any; it looks okay to me."

Therefore, a more helpful technique is to give the student specific directions about what is wrong. For example, "I see six problems wrong on this page—see if you can find them." Making your redirection very detailed gives impulsive students a *specific plan*, something they cannot generate on their own.

Goals
1. To reduce impulsivity
2. To improve self-management skills

Materials
Chalkboard
Overhead projector

Instructions

The student with ADD benefits from a plan or format for what will occur in class daily. Be sure you post your daily schedule and check off items as they are completed. This is equally important whether you have the student all day or for just one period. Provide individual schedules for students who may need copies to check off right on their own desks.

Variations

Example of a schedule for one 55-minute class period:

1. Transition time: 2 minutes

2. Review of yesterday's class: 5 minutes

3. Lecture: 20 minutes

4. Question time/Cooperative team time: 15 minutes

5. Homework assignment: 5 minutes

6. Review: 8 minutes

Independent Reading: Encouraging Concentration

Goals
1. To aid students in maintaining concentration and memory skills when reading literature
2. To improve self-management skills

Materials
Colored paper bookmarks (7" x 2", laminated)
Notebook rings
Hole punch
Felt-tip pens

Instructions

When the student is reading a book for English class, create a bookmark listing the basic steps in understanding the main idea and details in a story. Give the student a bookmark for each chapter of the book. Show the student how to put important information on the bookmark immediately on reading it.

On finishing the book, the student can place all the bookmarks on a notebook ring, creating a collection of notes about important material in the book. The bookmark can serve as a memory tool to help the student recall information about the book during a class discussion.

Here is a sample bookmark:

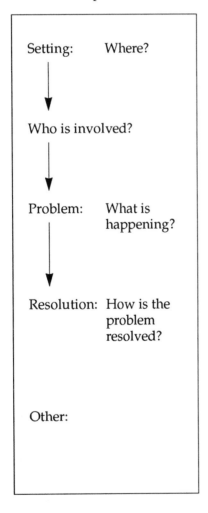

122

Independent Reading: Encouraging Concentration

Goals
1. To maintain concentration while reading content material
2. To improve self-management skills

Materials
Large colored paper clips
Textbook

Instructions

Students with attention concerns have a difficult time reading content material that is not intrinsically interesting to them. Suggest the following technique. It provides a "plan" for reading content, adds a gimmick for interest, and employs the strategy of using "covert" language to manage concentration.

Tell students to take the chapter they are to read and divide it into four or five manageable sections. At the end of each section, have them place a paper clip. Explain that if students become distracted or find it hard to concentrate as they read, they should repeat to themselves: "Read to the clip, read to the clip." On reaching the paper clip, they should put the book down and take a brief break before returning to the next chunk of reading. Each clip removed represents an accomplished task.

Students who have used this technique report that it helps them to know that they will have regular breaks as they read. In addition, it prevents them from constantly stopping to count how many pages they still have to read.

Variations
Post-it sticky tabs are also helpful for this task.

Color-Coding Technique: Foreign Language Vocabulary

Goals   1. To maintain concentration when learning vocabulary
              2. To improve self-management skills

Materials   Colored 3" x 5" cards

Instructions

Have students write vocabulary words they are learning on colored index cards. All nouns should be on one color, verbs on another, and so on. Keep the cards in a box divided by part of speech.

Variations

Place the cards on a notebook ring for quick review and practice sessions.

Have students draw simple illustrations on the cards to aid in recall.

Goals
1. To maintain concentration and memory when learning details in a content course
2. To improve self-management skills

Materials   Colored paper (9" x 12")

Instructions

As you introduce different facts and details in a social studies class, consider using pastel colored paper for the worksheets. Color code the sheets by categories to make the information easier to recall. For example:

- Important dates on yellow paper

- Concepts on blue

- Names of important leaders on pink

Variations

This color-coding technique aids in studying many pieces of information and can enhance recall on chapter or unit tests.

Mnemonic Technique for Recalling Vocabulary: The Keyword Method*

Goals
1. To maintain concentration and memory skills when learning vocabulary
2. To improve self-management skills

Materials   None

Instructions

This three-step method is introduced to help students recall vocabulary words and their definitions.

1. **Recoding:** The new vocabulary word is recoded into a keyword that sounds similar and is familiar to the student. The keyword should be one that the student can easily picture. For example, the keyword for the word "apex" might be "ape."

2. **Relating:** Create an interactive illustration, a mental picture or drawing, of the keyword interacting with the definition of the vocabulary word. Then formulate a sentence describing the interaction. For example: The ape is jumping off the top of Mt. Everest.

3. **Retrieving:** On hearing the new vocabulary word, students retrieve the definition by (a) thinking of the keyword, (b) remembering the interactive illustration or its sentence, and (c) stating the definition.

Variations

Place the words on index cards and illustrate the definitions with drawings.

---

* From Mastropieri (1988). Reproduced by permission of the author.

126

Mnemonic Technique: The Hand-Touch Method*

Goals   1. To use a mnemonic strategy for recalling key elements of a sentence
                  2. To improve self-management skills

Materials   Overhead projector
                  Drawing of hand on a transparency
                  Each finger is labeled for a feature of sentence construction:
                      1. Capital
                      2. Subject
                      3. Predicate
                      4. Complete Thought
                      5. End Mark

Instructions
Introduce students via the overhead to a visual and tactile way of using their fingertips to remind them of the key elements of good sentence structure.

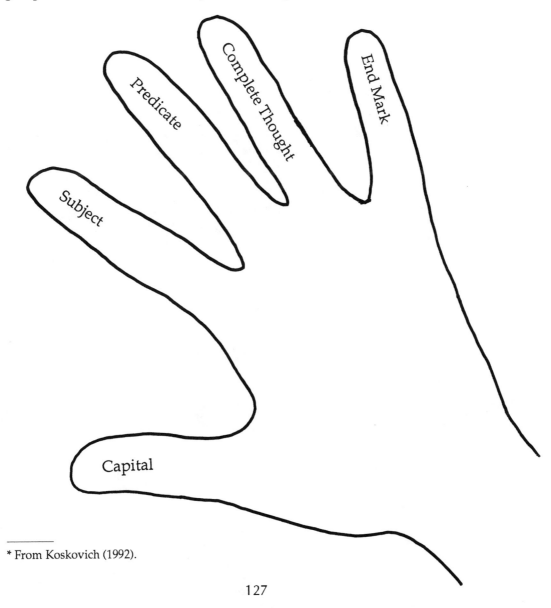

* From Koskovich (1992).

Goals   1. To improve listening skills
                2. To employ mnemonic strategies

Materials   Chart paper
                3" x 5" index cards

Instructions

1. Post the following mnemonic cue on a poster:

   T = Tune in: Be alert!

   U = Use your eyes; follow the teacher.

   N = Note-take; jot down facts.

   E = Encourage yourself to ask a question.

   I = Imitate strong role models in class.

   N = Now . . . you are tuned in!

2. Model the steps for students.

3. Have students make individual copies of the mnemonic on index cards to keep in their notebooks.

4. Employ the cue during lecture situations.

---

* From Jones (1993).

128

Memory Tricks: STORE the Story*

Goals
1. To improve comprehension, retrieval, and retelling of fiction or nonfiction by identifying consistent components
2. To employ mnemonic strategies
3. To provide a story frame

Materials
Chart paper
3" x 5" index cards

Instructions

1. Post the following mnemonic cue to help students improve their comprehension skills.

    S = Setting (Who? What? Where? When?)

    T = Trouble (What is the trouble or problem?)

    O = Order of events (What happens?)

    R = Resolution (What is done to solve the problem?)

    E = End (How does the story end?)

2. Model the steps for students.

3. Have students make individual cue cards on the index cards to keep at their desks during reading and writing tasks.

4. Review frequently during writing exercises.

5. Remind students to check the steps.

---

* From Schlegel and Bos (1986)

129

Goals   1. To increase monitoring for errors
            2. To employ mnemonic strategies

Materials   Chart paper
            3" x 5" index cards

Instructions

1. Post the following mnemonic cue to help students improve their proofreading skills:

    C = Capitals: first words in sentences, names of people, places, dates

    O = Overall appearance: fragments or run-on sentences, paragraph indentation, margins, marks, rips

    P = Punctuation: ends of sentences marked, commas

    S = Spelling: check

2. Model the steps for students.

3. Have the students make individual copies of the mnemonic on index cards to keep at their desks during writing tasks.

4. Review the COPS frequently during writing exercises.

5. Remind students to check the steps when writing a paper.

---

* From Schumaker et al. (1982).

Goals
1. To improve performance on teacher-designed tests
2. To employ mnemonic strategies

Materials
Chart paper
3" x 5" index cards

Instructions

1. Post the following mnemonic cue to help students improve their test-taking skills.

    S = Scan the test.

    U = Use a note card to block out sections.

    P = Place a mark next to questions you can't answer and move on.

    E = Exercise your brain; use mnemonic clues!

    R = Read carefully, check your work.

2. Model the steps for students.

3. Have students make individual copies of the mnemonic on index cards to keep at their desks during a test. Go over the strategies before test-taking situations and leave the cues posted throughout the test. Remind students to check the steps before handing in their tests.

---

* From Jones (1993)

Goals
1. To maintain concentration and memory skills when learning content
2. To improve comparison/contrast skills

Materials Photocopied format sheet

Instructions

Introduce a format to students which incorporates a plan for remembering and organizing thoughts when studying concepts. The format illustrated on the following page should be introduced to the entire class and rehearsed frequently. Make a photocopy of the format available for all students to use if they wish.

The Concept Diagram on the following page is an instructional tool used as part of the Concept Mastery Routine that was developed and researched at the University of Kansas Center for Research on Learning (Bulgren, Schumaker, and Deshler 1988). It is one of a number of teaching devices designed for teachers to use as they teach content information to classes containing diverse student populations. It is a data-based teaching instrument that has been found effective when used with a planning routine as well as a teaching routine that combines cues about the instruction, specialized delivery of the content, involvement of the students in the cognitive processes, and a review of the learning process and content material (Bulgren, Deshler, and Schumaker 1993). It has not been shown to be an effective tool if it is simply distributed to students.

---

* From Bulgren, Schumaker, and Deshler (1993). Reprinted by permission.

CONCEPT DIAGRAM

① CONVEY CONCEPT

Mammal ① **Vertebrate** ②

② OFFER OVERALL CONCEPT

③ **Key Words**

(elephant) (human)

warm-blooded

nurse the young

whale

bird

shark

walks on 4 legs

can fly

cold-blooded

③ NOTE KEY WORDS

④ CLASSIFY CHARACTERISTICS:

Always Present

warm-blooded	+
nurse the young	+
has hair	+

Sometimes Present

walks on 2 legs
walks on 4 legs
swims in water
can fly
moves on the ground

Never Present

0 cold-blooded

duckbill platypus

⑤ EXPLORE EXAMPLES

Examples:

(human)

(elephant)

(whale)

(bat)

Non-examples:

(snake)

(alligator)

(shark)

(bird)

⑥ PRACTICE WITH NEW EXAMPLES

⑦ TIE DOWN A DEFINITION

A mammal is a warm-blooded vertebrate that has hair and nurses its young.

A Strategy Checklist

Student's Name: _____

Date: _____

Goals
1. To help a team design an accommodation plan for a child with ADD in the classroom
2. To make the organization of strategies more efficient

Strategies
Indicate which strategies will be applied for this student.

____Give reinforcements/rewards

____Break work into small tasks

____Use multisensory approach

____Give physical contact

____Allow movement

____Provide extra chair to move to

____Write directions on card

____Have student dictate answers

____Use contracts

____Redirect

____Write out directions

____Give oral tests

____Rehearsal

____Check correct answers

____Use mnemonic devices

____Highlight sample problem on page

____Give immediate reward

____Allow work breaks

____Give checklists

____Provide bookmark for reading

____Include different tasks on worksheet

____Reduce copying from board

____SQ3R

____Read aloud when writing on board

____Teach study skills

____Record facts on rap tape

____Modify assignments

____Assign study buddy

____Avoid red ink and marking mistakes

____Give strong visual cues

____Give strong auditory cues

____Proximity _____ feet

____Allow more time

____Encourage peer modeling

____Have student dictate questions

____Needs eye contact

____Implement self-recording

____State objectives

____Give short tests

____Grade immediately

____Ignore fidgeting

____Have student complete checklist at dismissal

____Use alternate materials

____Circle key facts/directions

____Sequence tasks

____Give color cues

____Avoid colorful worksheets

____Provide card to cover parts of worksheet

____Reduce writing

____Reduce copying from book to paper

____Read, Cover, Recite, Check (RCRC)

____Teach subvocalization

____Teach relaxation techniques

____Use large spacing/double spacing

____Organize work into groups (chunking)

134

Chapter 6
A Case for Study Strategies

If Lindsay could go through life with her own personal secretary, I think she could make it . . . "Lindsay, here's your homework assignment." "Lindsay, here's a schedule of your tests next week." "Lindsay, I typed your report for you.". . . No, maybe a secretary isn't enough, an office manager would be better.

—Mother of a 14-year-old girl

I know it! I know it! Don't tell me, I'll remember. . . . Darn it! I can't remember, and I just learned it.

—16-year-old girl with ADD

Many students with attention disorders have difficulty with study skills and note taking. Their impulsive style hampers their test performance and their recall of information. We need to find ways to facilitate these academic skills. Here are specific recommendations that seem to benefit the majority of children with ADD/ADHD. These techniques are applicable to students in a wide range of ages.

Attention disorders often manifest themselves in school as a production deficit. The child fails to complete work, return assignments, or devote sustained attention to a task. Therefore, the student is unable to keep up within the daily classroom and very quickly falls behind. The most common reaction I hear from teachers regarding this child is: "If he would just keep up with his daily assignments, he could pass this class."

The first step to helping the child with attention difficulties experience success in the classroom is to change large tasks into smaller ones. Reduce the length, breath, and depth of homework lessons. Help the child by presenting assignments in small chunks and manageable doses. If a vocabulary list has 40 words to define and describe, have the student with attention difficulties cut the list in half. Ask yourself: "What is my goal in this lesson—quantity or quality?" Rehearsal—repeating problems or writing similar words over and over—is not the most concrete way for this student to learn. Often this student's workload can be reduced without reducing the benefit of the lesson.

The child's difficulties with planning and organization lead to struggles with recording homework, bringing home the appropriate books, and remembering to study for tests. The amount of time you can devote to teaching study skills may be limited. You may, however, be able to use student assistants to support you, to review study skills periodically, and to provide positive feedback to students who are struggling in these areas.

The statement we must direct to the student with ADD is not, "When will you remember to bring your homework back?" but rather, "How can I help you remember to bring your homework back?" It is well documented that the child with ADHD has poor cognitive planning skills. No amount of punishment, yelling, or negative consequences will change that. Retraining, coming up with other suggestions, offering other strategies for recall, *these* interventions are what can help the student become more productive. *Think of ADD/ADHD as a "production deficit"; these students just don't produce.*

Make your classroom an environment that models and reinforces good study habits and helps students complete their work.

1. Organize your own classroom in such a way that you provide times for recording homework and a group check that everyone has the assignment. (A sample format for recording homework is provided in figure 32.)

2. Set up one place where papers are returned. Color code it or identify it so students are well aware of its location. Set up an organizational strategy in which assigned students check to see whether all homework is in and report to you immediately.

3. Organize your lesson and provide outlines of the content or lists of key words. You can put the outline or list on paper, on an overhead transparency, or on a specially marked chalkboard or white board. Having a brief outline in front of them can help bring distracted children back to task.

4. When you present information that you feel is imperative for understanding, stop, point out, designate, and emphasize that the information you are about to share is vital and that students will need to record it. If the information is on the chalkboard or an overhead transparency, circle or star it. If you are presenting the material orally, make sure you pause while students copy down your comments.

5. As you teach, model note-taking skills on an overhead transparency or chalkboard.

6. Display around the room posters or cue cards that highlight specific study techniques and refer to them during your lessons.

7. Provide photocopied sheets with note-taking formats or beginning notes for a lesson to encourage the reluctant note-taker. Use diverse formats (see Figure 30 for suggestions).

8. Audiotape oral presentations and make tapes available for students who lack the skills to record notes proficiently. Provide carbon paper to a student who takes excellent notes and make the carbon copy available to students who have difficulty. Give the student extra credit for serving as a note-taker.

9. Allot time for a review of key points at the end of each lesson. This immediate class review will support the distracted student and reinforce all students' recall.

10. Post the homework assignment immediately after you give it. Have one area of the board designated for posting homework. Ask a student to read the assignment back to the class, or have the entire class read the assignment in unison.

11. Support your presentation with frequent gestures, visual animation, and enthusiasm. Pepper your conversation with vocal inflections and exciting vocal delivery. Use "active" illustrations and graphic interpretations as you speak.

12. Use technology to support your instruction—overheads, videotapes, demonstrations, and experiments can arouse students' interest.

13. Present material in well-defined clusters or chunks.

14. Avoid giving students long similar-appearing paragraphs of writing to copy.

15. Use sequential numbers, highlight phrases, or circle and box in important words.

16. Share positive comments regarding homework with students who have put special effort into their homework. For example, you might read from a particular homework assignment and feature one student's responses.

17. Periodically provide paper on which the homework assignment is to be done. Select colorful poster paper for a creative writing assignment or a bright fluorescent-colored sheet for a math assignment. This injects variety into a routine task.

18. Offer bonus points or incentives (example: homework coupons) for work returned on time.

Figure 29
Poster or Cue Card for Note-Taking

RULES FOR NOTE-TAKING

1. Use a note-taking format.

2. Highlight important points with colored pens, stars, arrows, and things like that.

3. Put a big question mark by anything you missed or didn't understand. Ask the teacher or a classmate to give you this information later.

4. Leave open lines and spaces on your note page so you can fill in additional material later.

5. Re-read your notes to yourself or with a friend within eight hours to help you remember them better.

137

Figure 30
Three Sample Note-Taking Formats

Format I

The Main Event (Idea):

This lecture was about:

V.I.P. Points:
1.   2.   3.

Format II

Topic

Information

Date

Questions

Format III

1. _____   1. _____

2. _____   2. _____

3. _____   3. _____

Topic

1. _____   1. _____

2. _____   2. _____

3. _____   3. _____

Calendars and Daily Planners

Because the student with ADD/ADHD has poor planning skills, daily planners, calendars, and other external aids become extremely important tools. Adults who provide a monthly or weekly calendar are using their environmental engineering skills to make the school experience ultimately more successful for this child.

1. Post a large planning calendar in the room or put one on an overhead transparency daily. Model how to record assignments, test dates, and other important events on the calendar.

2. Encourage the student to carry a daily calendar book. The type that is three-hole punched and fits into a loose-leaf notebook appears to be most efficient for the disorganized student.

3. Teach the student to color code or mark special due dates with a highlighting marker.

4. Calendars with hourly time schedules listed down the side work well for after-school planning. Students can break homework tasks down into small manageable time periods and include times for special activities (such as watching TV or making phone calls).

Figure 31
Sample After-School Study Schedule

	Monday	Tuesday	Wednesday	Thursday	Friday
3:00-3:30					
3:30-4:00					
4:00-4:30					
4:30-5:00					
5:00-5:30					
5:30-6:00					
6:00-6:30					
6:30-7:00					
7:00-7:30					
7:30-8:00					
8:00-8:30					
8:30-9:00					
9:00-9:30					

Figure 32
Sample Homework Recording Sheet

Name: _____   Week Of: _____

Monday	Tuesday	Wednesday	Thursday	Friday
Reading	Reading	Reading	Reading	Reading
P.E.	P.E.	P.E.	P.E.	P.E.
Math	Math	Math	Math	Math
Social Studies	Spanish	Science	Social Studies	English
Spanish	English	Social Studies	Art	Library
English	Music	English	English	
Science	Art	Spanish	Music	

Homework Recording Sheet

Name: _____   Week Of: _____

Monday	Tuesday	Wednesday	Thursday	Friday

Test-Taking Strategies

As often as eight out of ten times, students who have attention difficulties or a learning disability will know the correct answer on a multiple-choice test but will fill in the wrong bubble or space on a scan sheet. Their impulsivity and poor visual integration skills make this type of test format challenging for them. Try the following alternatives:

1. Allow the student to write the number or letter of the correct answer (A B C . . .) on a sheet of paper. Then grade the letters only.

2. Allow the student to write directly on the main copy of the test rather than having to use a separate sheet for recording answers.

3. Teach the student to place a ruler beneath the row of circles to be filled in so as to block out other rows on the scan.

4. Cover uncompleted portions of the test with a blank sheet of paper. Slide the paper down as each row is finished.

5. Demonstrate how to check carefully that the number on the answer sheet matches the number of the question before filling in the answer. Have the student practice as you supervise.

6. Teach your students to check the page number every time they turn a page. These students often rush through sustained test situations and are later penalized for missing a page or two.

General Accommodations

Maintain a positive atmosphere of success in your room for test-taking. Before your students start on a test, provide a slow stretching and deep breathing exercise. Give all students a blank piece of paper after they have cleared their desks. Tell them to use their paper to jot down anything they can remember that they have been studying. Let them use this page during the test. After all, everything they write down is from memory.

Impulsive learners have difficulty with multiple-choice questions. Because they have excellent gestalt skills and poor detail skills, they are often stymied by a multiple-choice format. After the test, they may feel they have done very well—in fact, they often state that they knew all the information. When the test is graded, however, they score poorly because they miss more complicated details in the questions. Suggest that these students learn to read the answers first, then read the question. Also teach them double-checking techniques.

Students with attention deficits should be encouraged to use their strong visualization skills in testing situations. Tell them that when they come to a problem they don't know the answer to, they should try to visualize the answer or picture when they watched the teacher give the information in class. This helps set up a chain for visual recall.

Test-taking accommodations may be necessary. A 504 accommodation plan may designate alternative methods that are more accurate indicators of a student's ability. The following options can be considered to maximize students' test performance.

Test-Taking Options for ADD/ADHD Students

1. **Taped response test.** The student may be allowed to tape responses to test questions rather than writing them out.

2. **Individual conferencing.** The teacher and/or an assistant designated by the teacher holds an individual conference to discuss the course. The adult may ask specific questions to which the student responds.

3. **Small-group tests.** Allow a small group of students to work together on a test—they can record their responses on tape or have one person write them.

4. **Teacher-read tests.** The teacher or a designated assistant reads the test aloud to the student. Responses may be written, given orally, or both.

5. **Essay test.** Give the student an essay test several days before the deadline. Allow the student to type the essay or to audiotape it. A scribe can then write out what the student said.

6. **Audiotaped tests.** Audiotape the test questions and allow students with ADD to listen on earphones as you read the test to the class. This helps reduce distractions for these students, and they can follow along as you read.

7. **Take-home tests.** Allow the students to complete the test at home or, for older students, during a study hall.

8. **Alternative project.** Students with ADD seem to do better on project-oriented activities. They may be allowed to do a project that they can demonstrate to the class. The project should illustrate their understanding of the content area.

9. **Study questions.** The student may be given study questions at the beginning of the unit and continue to use them throughout the unit of study. The final test then contains a representative sample of the questions from the study question list.

10. **Student-designed tests.** Ask each student to submit a few questions. Compile some or all of the questions into the class test.

11. **Chunking.** Always examine a test to see whether it can be broken down into more manageable chunks. Use highlighting markers to divide sections of the test. This will encourage the impulsive test taker to stop and look more carefully at the different parts of the test. Remember that this is a student who bores easily—use color, use tricks, use visual impact to trigger memory and recall.

Tricks of the Trade

In my private educational practice, I have a very successful program called *Back to School with Success* for students with ADD from elementary school through college age. This program takes place every year in August before school starts. I have found a variety of techniques that are very appealing to the inattentive learner. These "tricks of the trade" seem to benefit the students who employ them.

Study Tools for Students with ADD/ADHD

Clipboard. A clipboard is helpful in giving a sturdy base to a writing activity. If the child moves around frequently, the clipboard can provide a mobile surface for writing. It provides a "sense of security" for the student with ADD who at home typically prefers to study on the floor or in bed.

Electronic hand speller with dictionary. Children with ADD are often poor spellers. A hand-held electronic speller will attract the students' visual strengths, and they will remember the words more readily because of the visual imprint.

Because hunting for a word in a dictionary is often tedious and detailed work, these students find it difficult and boring. The hand-held dictionary is far more efficient and motivating to use.

Post-it Notes. Adhesive note pads should be in every student's backpack. These are helpful for writing quick messages, adding to homework lists, marking pages in books, and numerous other uses.

Post-it Tape Pop-Ups. Sticky tabs help the child mark pages, note homework assignments, mark important pages for tests, and the like.

Three-hole punch. Many of the papers that students receive during the day are not punched, and disorganized students tend to "jam" them into a notebook rather than sorting them. Having a hole punch encourages students to punch and organize their own papers.

Super-large three-ring notebook with colored inserts to divide subjects. Folders with pockets do not work well. The child adds and adds to the folder, eventually exceeding its capabilities!

Lightweight mechanical pencils and fine-tipped pens. For some students with ADD, writing is their least favorite task. They press so hard when they write that they are constantly having to sharpen their pencils. A disposable mechanical pencil is lightweight and provides a more fluid stroke. When they first start using a mechanical pencil, these students tend to break the lead frequently because of the pressure they exert. Eventually, most students learn to compensate and come to prefer a mechanical pencil or fine-tipped pen for writing.

Colorful stick-on dots. Students can stick colored dots on their personal calendars or on a classroom wall calendar to remind them of important upcoming dates and the like.

A small hand-held tape recorder. Students should have a tape recorder and supplies for audiotaping classes. The preferred model has a number counter on it. This way, when the student is recording a lecture and the teacher states, "This is important; it will be on the test," the student can quickly write the counter number on his or her notes. This facilitates finding the exact spot on the tape later on.

Colorful highlighting markers. A few different colors of highlighting pens are useful for marking notes and worksheets.

Index cards in a variety of colors. Students can use colored index cards to organize information quickly. For example, in studying Spanish, the student can write all feminine nouns on one color and all masculine nouns on another. For students with ADD, this adds a relevant cue to the memorization task.

Memory tape recorder. Some students like to use a small hand-held memory tape machine. Available for less than $30.00, these recorders are pocket-size and hold only about three to five minutes of tape. Students who are reluctant to write daily assignments carry these and record their assignments after each class.

Large, brightly colored paper clips. Colored paper clips tend to help the student who finds it difficult to read one chapter without daydreaming or constantly counting the pages to see how many are left. Have the student use paper clips to divide the chapter into chunks as described on page 123.

Personal organizational planners. A daily schedule calendar and appointment book on a hand-held computer is commercially available.

Additional Study Strategies

High-carbohydrate snacks. Students with ADD often experience cognitive fatigue when they remain too long with an activity requiring sustained attention. Proper amounts of sleep and a good diet are paramount. For students who are on medication, however, a snack late in the day after the medication wears off can help. Some students take a half dose of medication directly after school to help with study times.

Background noise. Some students with ADD are very successful having music, the television, or a ceiling fan on in the background to help them concentrate while they work. This background or "white" noise helps them tune out many different distracting sounds and concentrate on only one. Students in my study program also report success using tapes of environmental sounds or classical music as background noise. One student turns his room ceiling fan on high as he studies, finding the constant whirring helpful in tuning out other sounds.

Short study periods. Studying for small chunks of time appears to be more beneficial for the student with ADD than long study periods. Planning the study time to include enjoyable breaks can be motivating to the student. In setting up their schedules, students should be encouraged to consider and allot time for all types of activities, to schedule time for relaxation, and to set priorities for tasks based on their due dates.

Class schedules. As they get older and can participate in choosing their own class schedules, some students benefit from scheduling their core courses (basic skills) in the late morning, with high-interest classes later in the day. This tends to fit their "time clock" and make their day more productive.

Establishing priorities. People with attention deficits have lifelong difficulty distinguishing what is important to do right away and what can be done at another time. Lakein (1973) developed an ABC system that seems to be helpful in teaching students with ADD to set priorities. The ABC system requires that students list all the relevant activities—for example, all homework assignments—and assign each task a value:

> A = high value (have to do)
> B = medium value (should do)
> C = low value (can do tomorrow)

This system then identifies what the student should do first, second, third, and so on. The student crosses off each letter as the task is completed.

The SQ3R Method

Surveying, Questioning, Reading, Reciting, and Reviewing are the techniques in Robinson's (1969) reading study strategy that helps students recall information. Commonly known as SQ3R, this method provides students with a process that they can use primarily to read content material.

At first, students with ADD find this technique time-consuming because they are used to reading through a chapter very quickly. But if they can master the technique, they will see it really saves time because it eliminates their need to read a chapter over many times.

I. **Surveying** or scanning provides a general picture of what will later be studied in detail.

  A. First survey the whole book.
  1. Read the preface, foreword, and other materials addressed to the reader.
  2. Study the table of contents.
  3. Leaf through the book:
     a. Read summaries.
     b. Glance at headlines and topic sentences.

  B. Before reading each chapter, survey it.
  1. Read the headings.
  2. Reread the summary.

II. **Questioning** helps learning by giving it a purpose.

  A. Keep asking your own questions.
  1. At first write them down.
  2. Later, do this mentally after it becomes a part of your reading strategy.

  B. Use questions asked by the author.
  1. Use those in the textbook.
  2. Use those in the student workbook, if there is one.

III. **Reading effectively** means doing the following:

  A. Read actively, not passively, asking yourself periodically what you have learned.

  B. Note especially important terms.

  C. Read everything, including tables, graphs, and other illustrative materials.

IV. **Reciting** is a well-established aid to learning.

  A. It should be done while reading a book, in order to remember what is read.

  B. The amount of recitation done depends on the kind of materials.
  1. Up to 95 percent of memorization in studying is of disconnected materials such as rules, items, laws, and formulas.
  2. As little as 20 percent of studying is of well-organized storylike subjects such as literature or history.

V. **Reviewing** consists of repeating the steps above, plus the following:

  A. Resurveying the headings and summaries.

  B. Reread primarily to check yourself on how well you can recite.

Using Memory Aids

Students should become familiar with ways to associate new ideas and information with previously acquired information. Through association, students can increase their likelihood of remembering the new information. Two associative memory techniques that are useful are mnemonic devices and imagery.

Mnemonic devices associate what is to be remembered with a rhyme, an expression, or some other device. They need to be simple and clear to be effective. For example, "When two vowels go walking, the first one does the talking."

Imagery involves creating a mental picture that is exaggerated or absurd. Smith and Elliott (1979, 103) describe this technique as follows: "The student tries to picture a situation related to the material that is so outrageous or unlikely that the intensity of this association will evoke the recall required." As an example, a student might visualize hundreds of pigs going swimming as a key for recalling the "Bay of Pigs."

Learning Styles

Sandy is great at learning the multiplication facts—as long as she hears them first on a multiplication rap tape. "I need to hear it in a beat, then I remember it," says Sandy.

Kevin prefers a hands-on approach to learning. He remembers best by doing, especially something artistic or creative. He enjoys project-oriented tasks and works long hours to make them successful.

Sandy and Kevin are bright, enthusiastic students, yet each has a distinctive way of receiving and retaining information—a unique learning style. Students with ADD will benefit from understanding their particular modes of learning. We empower students when we help them recognize their own distinctive learning styles. When students recognize how they learn best, they can become their own best advocates in selecting teachers, choosing classes, and planning their academic activities.

Psychologist Howard Gardner (1987) identifies seven learning styles:

Linguistic. Children with a linguistic learning style develop strong auditory skills and often "think" in words. They enjoy poetry, stories, reading, and playing word games.

Logical/Mathematical. Logical/mathematical kids think conceptually and abstractly. They are able to see and explore patterns and relationships. They like to experiment, solve puzzles, and ask cosmic questions.

Spatial. Spatial learners think in images and are very aware of their environments. They like to draw, do jigsaw puzzles, read maps, and daydream.

Musical. Musical students are sensitive to sounds in their environment and they love music. They enjoy activities with a beat, rhythm, or pattern.

Kinesthetic. Children who are kinesthetic learners have a keen sense of body awareness. They are "tactile alert" and are very interested in movement. They enjoy making things, and they communicate well through body language.

Interpersonal. Children with strong interpersonal skills learn through interaction. They have many friends and are seen as "street smart." They have empathy for others.

Intrapersonal. Children with strong intrapersonal skills tend to shy away from others. They are very in tune with their inner feelings. They have strong wills, self-confidence, and opinions.

Help students discover their own learning styles. A child may have one dominant style or, more likely, a mix of several styles in varying degrees. Understanding and using one's learning style guides the child along the path of least resistance and greatest cooperation because learning springs from the child's own interests and aptitudes (Armstrong 1987). Here are some suggestions for teaching to different learning styles:

Linguistic. Encourage the child to study orally. Audiotape lessons; allow the child to study with others orally in groups. Teach computer skills. Use outlining as a study guide for this student. Link main ideas to visual images so the student can visualize concepts.

Logical/Mathematical. Teach through logical games, investigations, or mysteries. Teach comparison/contrast techniques. Use computers, games, and calculators.

Spatial. Teach using diagrams and visual cues. Present information at the student's eye level, not yours. Use visual aids and refer to them often. Teach through drawing, as well as verbal and physical imagery. Color code flash cards.

Musical. Clap out syllables and word parts. Show patterns, tapping out time in math problems. Use a stereo, radio, or metronome for timing. Audiotape assignments so the student can hear them. Use chants and choral reading exercises. Use a calculator with voice output.

Kinesthetic. Teach through physical activity and hands-on learning. Use role playing. Have the student trace words or letters in the air or on different surfaces.

How can you help your students identify their learning styles?

- Make up a questionnaire. Have students list their favorite and least favorite activities. Identify special talents, hobbies, and interests.

- Use commercially prepared learning inventories (see following selected bibliography).

- Observe what students are excited about, what types of things they enjoy learning, and what activities they choose spontaneously.

- Discuss with the students their observations of their own learning styles. Reinforce their styles of learning and encourage them to speak up regarding their preferred modes of instruction.

- Understand your own learning style. Try to incorporate other styles into your teaching repertoire in order to help all students. For example, if you tend to be strongly kinesthetic, make a point to add visual and verbal patterns to your instruction.

Remember that results of formal learning style measures should be considered informed guidance, not the final word. Follow up on testing with observations, verbal and nonverbal feedback, individual conferences, and other ways to confirm the accuracy of results.

Selected Bibliography of Learning Style Instruments

Learning Styles Inventory, by Joseph Renzulli and Linda Smith. Mansfield Center, CT: Creative Learning Press, 1978.

Learning Styles Inventory and Productivity Environmental Preference Survey, by Rita Dunn, Kenneth Dunn, and Gary E. Price. Lawrence, KS: Price Systems, 1981.

Myers-Briggs Type Indicator, by Isabel Briggs Myers and Katherine C. Briggs. Palo Alto, CA: Consulting Psychologists Press, Inc., 1976.

SRI Student Perceiver Interview Guide. Lincoln, NE: Selection Research, Inc., 1978.

Swassing-Barbe Modality Index, by Walter Barbe and Raymond Swassing. Columbus, OH: Zaner-Bloser, 1980.

Mnemonics

If we accept that all individuals learn in different ways, then we can accept that students need to learn different ways to remember. As we gain an appreciation of the variety of learning styles, we can respect individual differences and adapt our instruction to different situations. With students who have ADD, we must also be alert to situations in which their style may limit their success in the classroom. Mnemonics, symbols, or memory devices are excellent alternatives to the typical rehearsal method of memorization, and they are highly appealing to children who may have difficulty memorizing information.

Just how effective is mnemonic instruction? In a decade of research, students who received mnemonic instruction greatly outperformed controls taught by traditional instructional techniques. The foremost authority in mnemonic research, Dr. Margo Mastropieri, demonstrates that in classroom applications, student performance on content tests has more than doubled with the introduction of mnemonics.

Attention difficulties impair the memory ability of many children with ADD, which negatively affects their academic performance. Children who have difficulty with inattention may not be able to process several thoughts simultaneously or be able to store and retrieve that information quickly. Memory difficulties can impair their ability to recall letters of the alphabet, basic facts, phone numbers, and the like (recognition memory), despite repeated instruction. It is not unusual to encounter students with ADD in whom one or more of these retrieval processes is slow, variable, or inaccurate (Levine 1987b).

There are two types of memory: short-term memory and long-term memory. Short-term memory is a process of accumulating information quickly while concentrating on it. Levine identifies it as primary memory. Long-term memory is the process whereby information is stored after it has been repeated and processed with thoughtful attention. It is the vast accumulation of what we know (Jones 1991).

Children who are distracted by either visual or auditory factors typically have difficulty with short-term memory for visual and auditory information (Silver 1989). This difficulty is characterized by a "now they have it, now they don't" phenomenon (Telzrow and Speer 1986). Children with poor short-term memories may need other strategies to bypass their difficulty with recall. Mnemonics provide a sound "bypass" strategy as an intervention for this difficulty. Three types of mnemonics appear to work effectively with children who have attention problems:

- Rhythm (rhyme, beat or chant)
- Categorization or clustering (visual cues that highlight chunks of information)
- Association (making connections with previously learned material)

Once the mnemonics become a tool for learning, students can transfer this strategy to all learning situations and become progressively less dependent on a teacher. Mnemonics provide students a building block for developing a strong knowledge base. A strong knowledge base is a necessary first step to such higher-level skills as critical thinking and problem solving.

Selected Mnemonic Strategies

Because the child with ADD has stronger recall for information presented in chunks or clusters, the following mnemonics may be helpful in memorizing lists or other types of grouped information.

Acronyms. Make up acronyms where each letter represents the first letter of material in a word list. Examples:

- HOMES—each letter is the first letter of one of the Great Lakes: Huron, Ontario, Michigan, Erie, and Superior.
- STAB—the four voices in a quartet: Soprano, Tenor, Alto, Bass.
- Clusters of letters can also be used, as in Roy G. Biv (the colors of the rainbow); Ina V. Capp (parts of speech).

150

Acrostics. Acrostics are the opposite of acronyms, in that a sentence is invented to cue the retrieval of letters. The first letter of each word represents a target, a to-be-remembered letter. Examples:

- Every good boy deserves fudge (the notes on the lines of the treble clef).

- Grandmother England's old grandson rode a pig home yesterday (how to spell "geography").

- Please excuse my dear Aunt Sally (for recalling an algebraic formula: parenthesis, exponents, multiply, divide, add, subtract).

- My very educated mother just sent us nine pizzas (the nine planets in order).

Chanting. This technique employs a rhythm or beat for a rule that needs to be remembered; for example, phonics or language arts rules. The rule is presented in a chant or cheer format and is repeated again and again with rhythm and emphasis. Example:

- When two vowels go walking, the first one does the talking. First vowel, long vowel, say your name!

- Put two words together such as did and not. Take the "O" out of not, put an apostrophe in its spot. You have . . . didn't instead of not! (For learning contractions.)

- Have you heard? Oh have you heard? A word that shows action is a verb. You show the action when you say the verb. Run! Jump! Hop! (For recognizing verbs.)

The Keyword Method

In their book *Teaching Students Ways to Remember*, Mastropieri and Scruggs describe in detail a technique called the *Keyword Method*. This is a mnemonic tool for remembering vocabulary words and their definitions. It employs visualization and an acronym as its format. (The method is also described in the activities on page 126.) The Keyword Method is as follows:

Use three key steps to help you remember vocabulary words: Recode, Relate, Retrieve. Find the word you need to know and its definition. Then follow the next three steps using the three key words.

Recoding. First reconstruct the unfamiliar word into a similar-sounding keyword that is both concrete and familiar to the learner. A good key word for "apex" (which means the highest point of something) could be "ape," because it is visible in apex and is concrete enough to be easily pictured.

Relating. Once the keyword has been reconstructed and learned, it must be related or linked to the to-be-learned information. Combine the keyword and the definition. It is important that the keyword be doing something—interacting—with the definition. A good interactive picture for "apex" would be an ape jumping up and down on top of Mt. Rushmore.

Retrieving. To retrieve the definition, think first of the keyword, and then think of the picture. Finally, retrieve the definition from the information in the picture.

Remember to tell your students that the critical trick to this strategy is to make the word interact with its definition.

Rap Tapes

For the student who has difficulty remembering rote facts such as addition tables and multiplication tales, putting the fact into a rap-type lyric may help. Example: "3 x 6 don't be mean, 3 x 6 is just 18!" Rap tapes of math facts are available commercially, or you can make your own. Several resources are:

Addition, Subtraction, Multiplication, Division Rap Ups
written and produced by Mary Blakely
PACE, Inc.
7803 Pickering
Kalamazoo, MI 49002

Rock 'N' Learn Math Rap Tapes
DLM Teaching Resources
Now available from
SRA Technology Training Co.
155 N. Wacker Dr.
Chicago, IL 60606

Singing Multiplication Tables
by Hap Palmer
Educational Activities, Inc.

Also helpful are *Rhyme Times Cards.* They use clever rhymes and visual cartoons as mnemonics for math facts.

Rhyme Times Cards
by Carol Picard, M.A.
P.O. Box 28132
San Jose, CA 95159-8132

Math Rap
(author unknown)

3 x 6 now don't be mean,
3 x 6 is just 18.
3 x 7 is often done,
3 x 7 is 21.
3 x 8 opens the door,
3 x 8 is 24.
3 x 9 was made in heaven,
3 x 9 is 27.

4 x 5 is good luck plenty,
4 x 5 is merely 20.
4 x 6 is not a chore,
4 x 6 is 24.
4 x 7 finds a mate.
4 x 7 is 28.
4 x 8 is on my shoe,
4 x 8 is 32.
4 x 9 I can never mix,
4 x 9 is 36.

5 x 5, man alive!
5 x 5 is 25.
5 x 6 now don't get dirty,
5 x 6 is an even 30.
5 x 7 is on the hive,
5 x 7 is 35.
5 x 8 is really sporty.
5 x 8 is only 40.
5 x 9 has many wives,
5 x 9 has 45.

6 x 4 now try once more,
6 x 4 is 24.
6 x 5 is very flirty,
6 x 5 is merely 30.
6 x 6 I made from sticks,
6 x 6 is 36.
6 x 7 isn't new,
6 x 7 is 42.
6 x 8 is on the gate,
6 x 8 is 48.
6 x 9 can make me snore,
Cause 6 x 9 is 54.

7 x 4 never got a date,
7 x 4 is 28.
7 x 5 just took a dive,
7 x 5 is 35.
7 x 6 oh, guess who?
7 x 6 is 42.
7 x 7 gives me a sign,
7 x 7 is 49.
7 x 8 I wrote on bricks,
7 x 8 is 56.
7 x 9 is on the tree.
7 x 9 is 63.

8 x 8, and there aren't many more,
8 x 8 is 64.
8 x 9 do you know who?
8 x 9 is 72.

9 x 9 and we're finally done,
Cause 9 x 9 is 81.

Color Association

The effectiveness of using color to draw attention to relevant discriminative stimuli has been well documented (Zentall and Kruczek 1988). Using color has already been discussed in several other places, but as a review:

1. Use color to organize information into groups. Example: using color flash cards for remembering foreign language vocabulary—writing nouns on pink cards, verbs on green, and so forth.

2. Add color accents to key features of repetitive tasks that children with ADD often find boring and unmotivating.

3. Avoid adding color simply to increase the attractiveness of a task, especially for young, overactive children. If the task has not been overlearned, their performance may actually deteriorate (Zentall and Kruczek 1988).

Technology

Technology is part of today's classroom. Many electronic devices offer students with ADD ways to compensate for their skill deficits. Educators working with ADD often report that these students are very interested in computers and any video-related activity. Teachers relate that, whereas their students have difficulty staying seated through a class period, they are capable of long periods of sustained attention in front of a video game or computer screen. Computer technology can provide the compensatory strategies students need for success. Computer and video games attract children who have ADD for several reasons:

1. They respond best to activities that provide brevity, variety, and structure. Video games offer brevity in the sense that they contain short sequences with a minimum of delay. Novel and highly interesting software provides variety. At the same time, computer software operates within a structured format that has a clear operating routine and a defined beginning and end to each activity.

2. They are often very visual learners who respond well to the highly graphic format of video games and software.

3. They respond well to consistent and immediate reinforcement. Certain software programs contain a behavioral teaching component, in that they provide immediate reinforcement for learning a new skill. The programs are structured to repeat the material until the child has mastered the task. If the child needs more time to review the material on the screen, the response time can be adjusted. Computer programs offer self-paced activities that guide the child to developing independent work skills and may motivate the child to persevere.

4. Margolies (1990) suggests that many children with ADD maintain an illusory view of the world in which they are omnipotent. They may have a variety of related fantasies as self-protection against a world where they often fail. Video computer technology—especially video games—provide a creative fantasy environment where a child can feel in control.

5. Because many students with ADD are vulnerable to difficulties with short-term memory and attention to detail, their written language skills are weak. Spelling, punctuation, and grammar deficits may be part of their overall style. They benefit from spell-checking and grammar-checking software which proofreads for them and helps them correct errors.

Books on Tape

Audiotaped books are often helpful for students whose difficulties with attention hamper their comprehension. Students with excellent auditory recall skills can often repeat word-for-word information they have heard on a tape. Students like these will benefit from hearing a book on tape first, then scanning the actual book.

Many cassette tapes of popular books are commercially available. Many textbook companies also offer their texts on tape. If a student's reading comprehension is poor enough to prohibit him or her from being successful in school, the child may be eligible for books on tape provided by Recording for the Blind, Inc. A form describing the disability diagnosed by an educational therapist and a small registration fee are required. Upon acceptance, the student may receive any book requested free of charge.

Talking Calculator

This technological tool provides auditory input to a task that some students with ADD find visually distracting. The addition of auditory input helps their recall for the calculation task.

Figure 33
Product Resource List

Material	Product Name	Source
Spell Checkers, Dictionaries, Thesauruses	Franklin Learning Resources Product Line (hand-held)	Franklin Learning Resources 122 Burrs Road Mt. Holly, NJ 08060 (800) 525-9673
	American Heritage Dictionary	Houghton Mifflin Publishing Co. One Beacon St. Boston, MA 02108
Dictionary on computer	Franklin Add-on Software Dictionary (IBM)	Franklin Software 3511 N.E. 22nd Ave. Ft. Lauderdale, FL 33308 (800) 323-0023
Word Processor	Microsoft Word Version 5.0 (spell check, thesaurus, grammar check, outliner)	Microsoft Corporation One Microsoft Way Redmond, WA 98052-6399 (206) 822-8088 (800) 426-9400
Proofreading Software	Grammatik IV (IBM)	Reference Software 330 Townsend St. #123 San Francisco, CA 94107 (415) 541-0222
Outliner	Grandview (IBM)	Symantec Corp. 10201 Torre Ave. Cupertino, CA 95014-2132 (408) 253-9600
	Inspiration (Macintosh; graphic organizer)	Ceres Software, Inc. 2920 S.W. Dolph Court #3 Portland, OR 97219 (800) 877-4292
Personal Data Manager Software	WordPerfect Library (IBM) (menu/planner/notebook)	WordPerfect Corp. 1555 N. Technology Orem, UT 84057 (801) 225-5000
Personal "Stand Alone" Database	Texas Instruments Pocket Solutions Data Banks (hand-held)	Texas Instruments P.O. Box 53 Lubbock, TX 79408 (806) 747-1882
Free-Form Database	Info Select (IBM)	Micro Logic Corp. P.O. Box 174 Hackensack, NJ 07602 (210) 342-6518

156

Product Resource List (continued)

Material	Product Name	Source
Daily Schedule Planner	Day-Timers	Day-Timers, Inc. One Day-Timer Plaza Allentown, PA 18195-1551 (610) 266-9000
Books on Audiotape	N/A	Recording for the Blind 20 Roszel Road Princeton, NJ 08540 (800) 221-4742 (609) 452-0606

	N/A	Library of Congress
		National Library Service for
		  the Blind and Physically
		  Handicapped
		1291 Taylor St., NW
		Washington, DC 20542
		(202) 287-5100

Variable-Speed Tape Recorder	GE Handi-Cassette Recorder/Player	American Printing House for the Blind P.O. Box 6085 Louisville, KY 40206-0085 (502) 895-2405
Listening Aids	Easy Listener	Phonic Ear, Inc. 3880 Cypress Drive Petaluma, CA 94954-7600 (707) 769-1110 (800) 227-0735 Fax: (707) 769-9624
Voice-Output Calculator	Talking Calculator with clock and alarm	Sharp Electronics Corp. Sharp Plaza 20600 S. Alameda Street Carson, CA 90810 (310) 637-9488 Fax: (310) 603-9627

Books of Learning Strategies

Archer, A. 1990. *Study strategies for classrooms.* New York: Curriculum Skills Associates. (Books range from kindergarten to high school levels.)

Cornett, C. 1983. *What you should know about teaching and learning styles.* Cambridge, MA: Brookline Books.

Lakein, A. 1973. *How to get control of your time and your life.* New York: New American Library.

Mastropieri, M. A., and T. Scruggs. 1991. *Teaching students ways to remember.* Cambridge, MA: Brookline Books.

Scruggs, T., and M. A. Mastropieri. 1992. *Teaching test taking skills.* Cambridge, MA: Brookline Books.

157

Chapter 7
What Lies Ahead?
A Salute to the "Internal Spark"

Different is not defective.   From *You Mean I'm Not Lazy, Stupid or Crazy?*
                                                    by K. Kelly and P. Ramundo

Often when parents and teachers look at the characteristics of attention deficit hyperactivity disorder, they focus only on the deficits or the areas they perceive as weak. We need to affirm for the child with ADD/ADHD that indeed "you are okay, and if you can find your strengths, you can be successful."

As to the future, here is some food for thought: think about the active child who darts from one activity to another, the child whose internal clock is set on "go." This child could channel that energy into a career and leisure activities where intense movement is essential. Consider athletes, restaurant personnel, aircraft baggage handlers, salespeople, letter carriers, and disc jockeys. High activity is warranted and essential to people in all these professions. Just think about the activity level on the floor of the New York Stock Exchange! The active, restless child may mature into a young adult who has a wide range of interests. The child who can take this active style of learning and develop these various interests may become an adult complimented for his or her versatility!

There are capable adults who have attention disorders in every career imaginable, and they have been successful at every level. I know adults with attention disorders who are physicians, lawyers, teachers, fire fighters, and professional athletes. I have worked with adults with ADD who are entrepreneurs and head their own companies. Some are artists and some are photographers. What they have in common is ADD. What they *do not* have in common is what they choose to do with it.

When we work with young adults and parents who are experiencing the down side of ADD it is imperative to keep the positive factors in mind. I often use stories about famous people with ADD as encouragement and inspiration. In her book *Growing up Creative* Teresa Amabile salutes photographer Ansel Adams. Adams, known worldwide for his creative landscape photography, was a hyperactive child who had great difficulty adjusting to a traditional school environment. His father tutored him at home after Ansel had experienced several frustrating years in public school. Ansel's learning experiences were based on his activities and strengths. His father took things Ansel was intrinsically interested in and built the learning curriculum around them. In his autobiography, Ansel credits his father and salutes him for listening to his soul, the soul of a "different drummer." In his autobiography, Adams wrote:

I am certain my father established the positive direction of my life that otherwise, given my native hyperactivity, could have been confused and catastrophic. I trace who I am and the direction of my development to those years of growing up in our house on the dunes, propelled especially by an internal spark tenderly kept alive and glowing by my father. (Adams and Alinder 1990, 17)

Several years ago, a man in his late twenties came to my office to talk to me regarding his concern that he might have an attention disorder. He was feeling unsuccessful in his career. Although extremely talented with computers, he was always passed over for promotion in his department because of his poor organizational skills. Superiors recognized him as highly creative but felt that he would not succeed in a management position. They cited his difficulties with keeping to a schedule, his disorganization, and his impulsiveness as factors in denying him promotion.

These comments had plagued my client throughout his life—he had heard them before from his teachers and his parents. "You are bright," they told him, "but you just don't work up to your potential." One day my client watched an evening news special about attention deficit disorder. My client was intrigued; the descriptors read like an analysis of his personality. He began to read everything he could find on attention disorders, attended workshops, and finally came in to consult with me. After talking with him at length about his history, I urged that he seek a full evaluation to determine whether he indeed had ADD. Before the process began, I asked him to put into words how he felt at that time and what things, if any, he would change if he could. His response was, "I Wanna . . ." a selection I reproduced here with his permission. In this piece, we hear an adult describing what life with ADD is all about.

I Wanna . . .

I Wanna . . .

- Slow down.
- Be interested in people and what they say.
- Not feel the need to be in control of every situation.
- Ignore commercials on the radio.
- Accomplish what I set out to do instead of starting three other tasks.
- Reduce my frequency of auto accidents.
- Not change my lifetime goals hourly.
- Read a book and remember the story.
- Take notes at a meeting or a class that I can use later.
- Learn something from listening to a speaker and remember it.
- Not make a list every time I want to remember something.
- Be able to follow a list I've written.
- Enjoy traveling.
- Be satisfied with something I've done.
- Stop running from one hobby to another looking for fascination.
- Linger.

I Wanna . . .

- Pay attention to something that isn't intrinsically interesting to me.
- Build something from a plan without components installed backwards.
- Finish something I start out to do.
- Find peace without killing myself or anyone else.

My client was diagnosed with attention disorders and began on an intervention plan of counseling and medication. Many of the "I wannas" in his life are beginning to become realities.

There is increasing agreement in the research that at least a portion of the ADD population retain their difficulties into adulthood. Adults who had attention deficits as children continue to retain a relative deficit in the ability to learn but appear to be able to compensate for this difficulty through repeated exposure and practice (Klee, Garfinkel, and Beauchesne 1986).

Many adults with ADD/ADHD require assistance with educational choices or vocational planning. A counselor, parent, concerned adult, or friend can help them to achieve a realistic understanding of their strengths and how to match these to career choices.

Steps to Success

Convincing adults with ADD that their problems stem from neurological or biological causes rather than a defect of character or laziness is often the first step in improving their self-esteem. Two adults who have ADD, Kate Kelly and Peggy Ramundo, wrote a book, *You Mean I'm Not Lazy, Stupid or Crazy?* In it, they share their philosophy that "different is not defective." Reading about ADD and other adults who cope with it can lay the foundation for accepting and overcoming this condition. (A list of adult resources begins on page 168.)

The second step is to have both a psychological and an educational diagnostic test of abilities and achievement levels. This diagnostic battery serves as a blueprint for academic and career choices. It can also indicate whether medication is likely to be helpful. The third step is implementing behavioral strategies that can help the adult combat deficits and feel organized and in control. Figure 34 includes some suggestions for adults who are living with ADD.

Vocational School Options

Post-secondary vocational programs are an option for many students who are not interested in a college education but want the professional training that leads to marketable skills and a job future. Vocational education is defined by Scheiber and Talpers in their book *Unlocking Potential* (1987) as "education geared for employment, but not a baccalaureate (B.A./B.S.) degree." Vocational graduates earn either a degree or a certification in a particular area. Vocational education programs are available in both public and private institutions, and programs exist in hundreds of occupational areas. These programs teach skills ranging from aviation to hotel/restaurant management, from forestry and agriculture to upholstering.

An evaluation of vocational skills and abilities is an invaluable aid. This type of evaluation is available through a public high school or can be done by a private vocational evaluation agency.

Because people with ADD tend to be impulsive decision makers, they need to rely on input from counselors, friends, and teachers regarding career choices. They should be guided to select a career for its long-term benefits, not its immediate appeal. The vocational evaluation will certainly pinpoint talents and give the person direction for making a wise choice. Some suggestions are given in Figure 35.

Figure 34
To the Adult Who Has Attention Deficits

1. Keep an appointment book or planning calendar. If you find it difficult to write, keep a calendar on computer.

2. Every morning, make a list of what you want to accomplish that day and keep it with you at all times.

3. Place pads of Post-it Notes in strategic places so you can jot down thoughts immediately.

4. Carry a portable tape recorder and record important dates, times, and other things you need to remember.

5. Place an oversized calendar on a prominent wall in your home. Color code dates and important meetings.

6. Take a course in study skills and strategies if you are a student. If you are working, take a time-management course. Tape the course and listen to it as you drive to work in your car.

7. Break down tasks you must accomplish into small steps. Take a report or project and divide it into manageable chunks.

8. Use colored paper clips or colored file folders to organize your written material into well-defined groups.

9. Employ desk organizers, briefcases with file inserts, file cabinets, boxes color coded by subject, bulletin boards, and shelf systems to add structure and order to your life.

10. Make a list of goals for yourself. Set a daily goal—and make it simple. When you achieve your goal, reward yourself with something you enjoy or find rewarding. For example: "If I can write my assignments down all day long, on my way home after class, I'll stop and buy a frozen yogurt."

11. Reduce or eliminate alcohol or drug use. Plan periods of exercise or "mind escape activities"—movies, video games, and the like—as a distraction when you feel challenged.

12. Work at eliminating negative "I" messages you give yourself. These self-deprecating comments are the result of years of verbal abuse and negative reactions from ignorant people. You don't need another voice pulling you down! Stop those statements when they start and substitute positive messages. Instead of, "Oh no, I did it again—I interrupted the boss—I am such a jerk." Replace that with, "I did accomplish something, my point was expressed. And the boss did like the idea."

162

To the Adult Who Has Attention Deficits (continued)

Kevin Murphy, Ph.D., at the University of Massachusetts Medical Center, urges adults with ADD to become their own best friends. He suggests that self-affirming comments are the first step to recovery.

Following this list of suggestions will take hard work. Often people with ADD have to work harder and expend more energy than their fellow students or co-workers.

In the Fall/Winter 1992 special edition of *CHADDER*, one article particularly brings into focus the extra effort required for a person with ADD to be successful. An adult who is a reporter and also has ADD is interviewed. This man (who is not identified by name) shares some of the compensatory strategies he has used throughout his ten-year career as a reporter for a medium-sized metropolitan daily newspaper. Here are some of his coping skills:

> How do I, as an ADD adult, manage my career as a reporter?
> - I tape record all interviews.
> - I prepare a list of questions in advance of each interview.
> - I carry photocopies of information I may need to refer to.
> - I use a computer to correct my spelling and help with note taking.
> - When I'm on the phone, I plug the other ear.
> - I underline and bracket key parts of what I read.
> - I use a copy stand with attached sliding ruler to keep my attention from jumping from line to line.
> - I get some kind of physical exercise daily.
> - I drink lots of coffee.

The author also takes a medication, Norpramin (desipramine hydrochloride), which combats depression, anxiety, and the desire to drink alcohol. This combination of steps has been an extremely successful intervention for the man who wrote the article. It certainly documents the fact that preparation, planning, and practice are key elements to success.

Figure 35

Tips for Students with ADD/ADHD Who Are Selecting a Vocational Education Program

1. Choose a school that offers specific support services. Ask whether tutors are available at the site (or whether the school can provide a list of tutors).

2. Select a school where faculty members are available to students. You will need direct contact with your instructors. Instructors at some vocational schools have full-time jobs in addition to their position at the school and may not be very accessible.

3. Select a school that states it is willing to make accommodations for students with special needs. Examples are untimed tests, note-taking services, and audiotaping of classes.

4. Purchase your equipment, materials, and books well before going to the first class. Become familiar with the equipment by name and sight. Scan the books before you enter class to help you recall information.

5. Use a variety of study tips and mnemonics to help you recall information.

6. Speak with your instructors on a regular basis. Be honest about your limitations and strengths. You may want to meet with instructors prior to each class to review material and increase your chances of succeeding in the class.

7. Be aware that you are making a financial investment when you enter a vocational program. Ask yourself, "Am I sure I will be able to learn the skills being taught?"

8. Your attention deficit disorder is a private issue. It is your choice whether you share that information with your instructors. If you are taking medication, be aware that you may be involved in drug checks on the job. You will want to discuss with a counselor how this situation should be handled.

The College-Bound Student with ADD/ADHD

A high-school graduate with ADD may wish to go on to college and have the ability to do so, but college entrance exams can be an obstacle. People with ADD typically score poorly on standardized tests. I have observed students having difficulties for the following reasons:

Impulsivity. Students see part of a question and quickly answer it without reading the complete answer.

Anxiety. Test taking is anxiety producing for students who have difficulty with recall and short-term memory.

Gestalt orientation. These students have great gestalt skills and could do well on an untimed, essay-type test. But they do poorly with multiple-choice formats because of their repetitiveness and the attention to detail they require.

164

Become a Professional Test-Taker!

To feel more confident on these test measures, students with ADD need opportunities to become very familiar with the test format. They will benefit from taking practice tests. Practice copies of college entrance exams are available in most bookstores, and students can randomly test themselves on different sections. They can also enroll in workshops or classes that review the test and provide help in understanding its format.

Several commercially available books about the SAT/ACT exams have "hit" lists of vocabulary words that have been used frequently on the exams. They provide an excellent review. SAT/ACT review software is also helpful. Working on a computer is visually appealing, so practice may seem less tedious. See the resource list at the end of this chapter for SAT and ACT preparation software.

Figure 36
Tips for Students with ADD/ADHD
Who Are Selecting a College Program

---

1. Have a thorough educational diagnostic evaluation before you head to college in order to determine your strengths and weaknesses as a student.

2. Choose a college or university where class sizes are small and there are more opportunities for direct teacher contact.

3. Consider a school that operates on the quarter rather than the semester system. Many students do better with consolidated and intense courses over a shorter period of time than with semester-long courses that require longer periods of sustained attention.

4. Select a school that has a strong system of support services. An important service is on-campus tutoring available at low cost. Particularly appealing are schools that offer services for students with learning disabilities.

5. Select your instructors based on *your* strengths. If there are two freshman English professors, find out about their teaching and testing styles. Seek out teachers who are known for using highly visual presentations (overheads, diagrams, models) and have dynamic personalities. Look for classes in which your grade is based on a variety of different testing formats and projects. You will be more successful with a variety of testing procedures rather than, for example, only multiple-choice tests.

6. If you don't have a computer to take to college, begin saving for one. Or select a school with an all-night computer lab that is accessible to your housing.

7. Visit the campus a month before classes start. Walk the common areas; know where the library, tutoring center, and computer center are. Become intimately familiar with the campus before school starts.

8. Where you live is an important factor. Avoid large dorms, if possible. Room alone if you can't find a roommate who is well organized and responsible. You need strong models in your life and will be hindered by a roommate who is also challenged by lack of focus.

165

Hanging in There

Now, how about *staying* in college? Here are some suggestions to help you remain in school and complete that degree!

1. Take manageable course loads every semester. Don't take 19 hours just to get through faster. Opt for manageable course loads of 12 hours or so.

2. Organize your desk and study area. Make sure your desk doesn't face a window. Have all your materials readily accessible.

3. Be prepared with compensatory strategies; use electronic and computer technology. Have a computer, tape recorder, electronic hand-held speller, electronic day scheduler, and calculator—and always carry extra batteries.

4. Be prepared with important study gimmicks. Try these organizers:
   - Colored note cards
   - Post-it Tape Tabs and Notes
   - Clipboard
   - Three-hole paper punch
   - Large notebook rings
   - Large three-ring binders
   - Color-coded folders and files

5. Rely on and use support services, tutors, and study buddies on campus. Sign up for study groups before tests, or start your own. You will work harder if you study with a highly focused fellow student.

6. Obtain notes from other students in your classes to supplement your notes and to review other thoughts on the same topic.

7. Audiotape classes and play back the tapes when you are relaxing or exercising on a stationary bike.

8. Have a large bulletin board and calendar in your room and constantly check to see that you have recorded all your assignments and due dates.

9. Have a friend read your syllabus for each class and make sure that you have accurately recorded the dates of all upcoming tests and reports.

10. Use cartons and discarded grocery boxes to set up an organized storage system in your room for papers, assignments, and such things. Color code the boxes by subject or course.

11. Meet and greet your professors. Stop in before and after class. Set up appointments with them before tests. Review tests and assignments with them. Don't be an anonymous student in their classes. Show them you are trying your best to be a conscientious, successful student.

12. Believe in yourself! Post self-affirming statements on your bulletin board to motivate and inspire yourself. "Just do it!"

Growing Up ADD/ADHD

Seven years ago, I received a phone call from an elementary school principal. He said, "I read an article you wrote on attention deficit disorder. Don't you know it's just a yuppie disorder?" I knew I had my work cut out for me.

For those of us who work with clients who have attention deficits, there has never been any doubt that the disorder exists. I can sit with a mother and hear her describe life with her ADD son. An hour later, I will sit with another mother from another part of town and hear almost word-for-word the same description of her daughter. This commonality of difficulties is staggering but ever-present and always, always real.

For me, the most challenging part of my practice involves actual work with clients. My clients are always special, exciting, and intense. Most of them have a wonderful inner spark that I feel fortunate to glimpse when I work with them. At the end of an evaluation, when we are sharing the results and I am describing to them what I think their life must be like, they often exclaim, "That's me! *How* did you know I do that?"

When I first became part of a multidisciplinary team diagnosing attention deficits, I was concerned about how students would feel and how their parents would react to the diagnosis. I thought, "What are we doing? Setting off a box of fireworks?" But the reaction is never explosive. The diagnosis is often received with relief and affirmation. Many families tell us, "We just knew something was causing this. Now let's move on to doing something about it!"

I also am very aware of the lifelong implications of attention disorders. Although the challenges are different at each age level, they are omnipresent. Serving students with attention disorders often means seeing them periodically as they mature. It means helping them develop strategies and coping skills for a variety of events throughout their lives. The preschooler whose parents we helped with parenting skills becomes the elementary student who requires a social skills program and a middle schooler who needs study skills. The high schooler returns for test-taking strategies, tutoring, and career guidance. The intensity of the difficulties varies at each stage, but the disorder is present throughout the person's life span. Understanding how ADD is likely to affect a person at different ages helps us envision a true perspective of "growing up ADD" (see Figure 37).

Figure 37
Life History of Attention Deficits

Infant	Temperamental dysfunction, insatiability, irritability, unpredictability, feeding or sleeping problems, colic
Toddler	Unusual overactivity, preschool adjustment problems, crankiness, irritability, extreme insatiability
Elementary Schooler	Impaired focus, distractibility, impulsivity, inconsistent performance, possible hyperactivity, weak short-term memory, visual motor integration difficulties
Adolescent	Restlessness, inconsistent performance, impaired focus, memory problems in school, frustration
Young Adult	Vulnerability to underemployment, automobile accidents, substance abuse, difficulty with relationships
Mature Adult	Concentration problems, impulsiveness, poor frustration control, tendency to interrupt, restlessness, impatience, poor response to stress, easily irritated

This information is compiled from data obtained from Jones (1991) and Levine (1987a)

Resources for Adults and Young Adults with ADD/ADHD

Kelly, K., and P. Ramundo. 1993. *You mean I'm not lazy, stupid or crazy?* Cincinnati, OH: Tyrell and Jerem Press.

Weiss, G., and L. T. Hechtman. 1986. *Hyperactive children grown up.* New York: Guilford Press.

Weiss, L. 1992. *Attention deficit disorder in adults.* Dallas, TX: Taylor Publishing.

Wender, P. 1987. *The hyperactive child, adolescent and adult: Attention deficit disorder through the life span.* New York: Oxford University Press.

Support Groups and Organizations

ADDult Support Network
Mary Jane Johnson
2620 Ivy Place
Toledo, OH 43613

Attention Deficit Resource Center
Lawrence L. Melear, Ph.D., Director
1344 Johnson Ferry Road, Suite 14
Marietta, GA 30068
(800) 537-3784

The National Institute for Attention Deficit Disorder (NIADD)
Peggy E. Ramundo, Executive Director
407 Resar Avenue
Cincinnati, OH 45220

Resources for Adults (continued)

Children and Adults with Attention Deficit Disorders (CH.A.D.D.)
499 Northwest 70th Avenue, Suite 308
Plantation, FL 33317
(305) 587-3700

There are local support groups in every state, plus some foreign countries. Local groups meet once or twice a month, and are open to both members and nonmembers of CH.A.D.D. Call the National Office for information on contacting a group in your area.

Learning Disabilities Association
4156 Library Road
Pittsburgh, PA 15234
(412) 341-1515

Learning Materials

Hand-Held Spellers
Available commercially through Franklin Company and Texas Instruments; an American Heritage Dictionary Hand-Held Speller is also available.

Hand-Held Day Schedulers
Available through Sharper Image Stores and office supply stores such as Biz Mart and Office Mart

Hand-Held Tape Recorders
Look in electronic retail stores (Radio Shack, Olsen)

Catalog of Books and Videotapes
A.D.D. Warehouse
300 Northwest 70th Avenue, Suite 102
Plantation, FL 33317
(800) 233-9273

Post-it Tape Tabs and Post-it Notes
Available at stationery and drug stores everywhere.

SAT/ACT Software
Interactive Learning Systems, Inc.
6153 Fairmount Avenue, Suite 213
San Diego, CA 92120
(619) 283-8760

Books on Audiotape
Recording for the Blind, Inc.
20 Roszel Road
Princeton, New Jersey 08540
(609) 452-0606

If you qualify as learning disabled or visually impaired, you are eligible to receive audiotaped books free of charge.

Talking Books
National Library Service for the Blind and Physically Handicapped (NLS)
The Library of Congress
1291 Taylor Street, N.W.
Washington, DC 20542
(202) 882-5550

Magazines, abridged classics, and popular novels are available free of charge if you have a specific reading disability.

Resources for Adults (continued)

Newsletters for Adults

ADDendum
c/o CPS
5041-A Backlick Road
Annondale, VA
4-issue yearly subscription is $12.00.

ADDult NEWS
Mary Jane Johnson, Editor
2620 Ivy Place
Toledo, OH 43613
4-issue yearly subscription is $8.00.

The ADDvisor
Attention Deficit Disorders Association
19262 Jamboree Blvd.
Irvine, CA 92715
(800) 487-2282

Electronic Newsletters (Bulletin Boards)

America On-Line®—Disabilities Forum
Prodigy®—ADD Bulletin Board

Vocational Resources

Call your state Department of Education and ask for the office of the Director of Vocational Services.

National Association of Vocational Education Special Needs Personnel (NAVESNP)
American Vocational Association
2020 14th Street
Arlington, VA 22201
(703) 522-6121

National Center for Research in Vocational Education
1960 Kenny Road
Columbus, OH 43210
(800) 848-4815

Chapter 8
What the ADD/ADHD Team Process Really Is: Case Studies

> In order to make a differential diagnosis of Attention-Deficit/Hyperactivity Disorder, the practitioner needs to evaluate a variety of situational and medical factors.
>
> —From *Managing Attention Disorders in Children*
> by S. Goldstein and M. Goldstein (1990, 157)

In talking with diagnostic teams and child study teams throughout my state and other states, I have had multiple requests for models or samples of case studies. A model is often helpful in writing a report. For that reason, in this chapter I provide a variety of case studies. The first two case studies are multidisciplinary in nature, representing reports that include medical intervention and are generated by a team of professionals. The third study represents a psychoeducational diagnostic model. The final four case studies are examples of educational diagnostic assessments.

These reports have been prepared with concern for maintaining client confidentiality. Therefore, all identifying information has been changed, and all information regarding culture, race, or ethnicity has been eliminated.

Case Study	Type
Pat M.	Multidisciplinary Evaluation
Ben F.	Multidisciplinary Evaluation
HC	Psychoeducational Evaluation
JD	Educational Evaluation
MM	Educational Evaluation
JG	Educational Evaluation
MB	Educational Evaluation

Sections of a Diagnostic Report

These paragraphs summarize the sections that are generally included in a diagnostic report and give the type of information that may be covered in the sections. Although each school or clinic is likely to have its own format for reports, most will be similar to the samples given here.

1. **Medical History.** The importance of a complete medical history is well recognized in clinical practice. Although this is especially true for children with acute medical difficulties (for example, head injuries) a comprehensive med-

ical history may also be contributory when evaluating children who show signs of attention disorders. In addition, a complete vision and hearing screening should be completed. A systematic medical history may identify other circumstances or anomalies that are relevant to interpreting test data. I consider The *ANSER System* (Levine 1985) an exemplary history-taking system, and I used it in preparing the case studies in this section.

2. **Early Development History.** This information can reveal difficulties with attention and concentration in preschool or nursery experiences. In addition, through comparing gross motor and fine motor milestones with cognitive and linguistic process, patterns of difficulty might be identified. Histories of allergies and chronic ear infection are significant for ADD.

3. **Family History.** Family history information regards psychiatric history (that is, depression and other mental illness), as well as history of alcoholism. It looks at family learning styles and physical histories of family members (for example, thyroid deficiency).

4. **Psychoeducational Assessment.** The psychometric evaluations include tests of ability and achievement. In some cases, tests of coordination, motor ability, and language assessment are included.

5. **Observation.** The student should be observed in a setting outside of the test-taking situation. The child should be observed in the classroom, on the playground, during lunch period, in gym, and during music or art classes.

6. **Recommendations/Interventions.** Intervention with attention deficit children involves a multimodality process. The recommendations made in this section of the report start the treatment program in motion. The initial evaluation serves as the "blueprint" for intervention. The educator can use this "blueprint" to design classroom strategies that maximize the child's learning potential. The educator should match teaching approaches to a child's strengths. In addition, the educator can suggest compensatory techniques and materials which can also assist the child in developing self-management and coping skills. We need to avoid treating attention deficit as if it were a behavioral problem and approach it from the direction of how we as a team can help a student cope with the disorder and move ahead successfully with interventions.

SAMPLE REPORT 1

Multidisciplinary Team Evaluation

Case: Pat M.

DOB: 11/17/81

We had the opportunity of seeing Pat M., age 7¹/₂ years, in the Child Diagnostic Program on June 1. Pat was accompanied today by his mother. He has completed the first grade at Fairview Elementary School. Concerns center around his difficulties in getting his schoolwork done and in behaving appropriately with peers, both at school and at home. He has been evaluated in the past, and Cylert 37.5 mg. had been initiated. The dosage was subsequently increased to 75 mg. per day. The medication, which was discontinued at the end of the school year, apparently did have some success in changing his behaviors at home and improving his eye-hand coordination. Ongoing academic difficulties were noted, however. His teachers have consistently expressed concern that inattention in the classroom has interfered with his ability to perform appropriately.

Pat is described as being a very optimistic child who is viewed by his mother very positively. He is an affectionate, kind, and sympathetic youngster who socializes very well. His mother is concerned as to whether he does indeed have an attention deficit disorder, what treatment would be appropriate for him at this point, and what appropriate expectations for him would be.

Pat has been attending psychological counseling on a monthly basis since his initial diagnosis. This therapy has been helpful both for Pat and for his family members, because the counselor has been very supportive within the counseling situation and within the home setting.

Background Information

Pat was adopted soon after birth. He was born full-term, weighed 8 1/2 pounds, and had no significant neonatal problems. He was placed in foster care at birth, where he remained for eight months before being adopted by Mr. and Mrs. M.

Pat's health has always been good, with the exception of frequent episodes of otitis media and slow weight gain. Functionally, he was remembered as being an easygoing youngster who nonetheless was always very active. He has had trouble falling asleep and was difficult to comfort and console.

Pat was fully bowel and bladder trained by the age of 2 years, and no problems have persisted in this regard. Mr. and Mrs. M. feel that Pat's gross and fine motor abilities are age appropriate and that he has no difficulty with either expressive or receptive language.

Pat is often difficult to satisfy and frequently demands excessive physical attention. Mrs. M. has always felt some concern about Pat's difficulty with attention. She commented that he often notes things that are out of the ordinary and has trouble concentrating in large groups. He seems to have too much energy, and his body is in motion most of the time.

School Information

Information was obtained from the school in the form of a questionnaire completed by his teachers. They note that he has a short attention span and he has limited on-task behaviors. His academic performance is lower than expected for his age. His teachers are concerned about how they might keep him still for longer than 30 seconds. They feel that he needs to consider the consequences of his behaviors. They note that his reading ability is above age expectancy, although he does have some difficulty with writing.

The *ACTeRS Questionnaire* was completed by his teachers, who report that he persists at tasks for short periods of time and has difficulty in completing assignments independently. He also has difficulty in following multistep instructions. He is almost always on the go, fidgety, and restless in his seat.

Clinical Evaluation

Pat separated easily from his mother for today's assessment by Dr. C., developmental pediatrician. His height was 48 inches, and his weight 45 pounds. His head circumference was 50.5 cm. No significant dysmorphic features were evident on physical examination. Neurological examination did not reveal any focal or lateralizing findings. Deep tendon reflexes were equal and adequate bilaterally. Pat was a very open and social child who was very mannerly, pleasant, and interested in the examination procedure. He was very impulsive, fidgety, and yawned frequently. He often asked when the examination would be completed.

Pat was able to visually track horizontally and vertically without any difficulty, and he had good near-point focusing skills as well. Fine motor skills were felt to be age appropriate, and he had no difficulty in imitating finger movements (propriokinesthetic functioning). His ability to perform rapid alternating movements of his forearm was also age appropriate. He was right-dominant in his hand, foot, and eye.

Pat had no difficulty with tasks involving sequencing of auditory or visual information. As far as language skills are concerned, Pat's receptive language functioning, measured by the *Peabody Picture Vocabulary Test,* was above age expectancy at a standard score of 116 on Form M. Expressively, no concerns in regard to syntax were noted. His performance on the *Boston Naming Test,* a test measuring word-finding abilities, was also within normal limits for a youngster of his age. During the course of conversation, some developmental misarticulations were evident, especially with "th" and "r" sounds.

Psychological Evaluation

Pat was evaluated by a child psychologist, Dr. C. Pat appeared to function appropriately for a 7-year-old boy. Interpersonally, he was friendly and cooperative and showed a delightful sense of humor. Pat displayed a very high activity level throughout the session. He constantly squirmed in his seat and, by the end of the session, was leaving his seat regularly.

In his working style, he showed an interest in new tasks and was generally persistent in problem solving on a one-to-one basis. On less structured tasks involving less interaction with the evaluator, he showed marked difficulty in monitoring his own work. Results of the coding subtest were discarded in the calculation of performance IQ because Pat had a very short attention span and failed to complete the tasks presented. It was felt that today's results might yield a low estimate of Pat's functioning.

Tests Administered

Draw-a-Person
Personality Inventory for Children
Wechsler Intelligence Scale for Children—R

Verbal Tests	Standard Score
Information	11
Similarities	13
Arithmetic	9
Vocabulary	17
Comprehension	11
Digit Span	(16)

Performance Tests

Picture Completion	12
Picture Arrangement	16
Block Design	11
Object Assembly	11
Verbal IQ	113 ± 7
Performance IQ	118 ± 8
Full-Scale IQ	118 ± 6

Psychological Findings

Today's cognitive assessment using the *Wechsler Intelligence Scale for Children* showed Pat to be functioning in the high-average range, with a full-scale IQ score of 118. This score was based on a verbal IQ score of 113, and a pro-rated performance IQ score of 118, both also in the high-average range. These results suggest that Pat has the potential to perform at or above grade level on national normed academic tests.

In verbal subtests, Pat showed superior strength in his general vocabulary skills. He was above average in his verbal abstract reasoning skills, as well as on short-term auditory memory and sequencing abilities.

On performance tasks, he showed a strength in his social problem-solving skills and visual sequencing.

Social/Emotional Screening

When asked to draw a picture of a person "doing something," Pat produced a drawing of a Nintendo character jumping over a bridge.

Inquiry questions revealed that Pat feels loved and supported by family members. Other questions revealed age-appropriate interests and concerns. Pat showed himself to be sympathetic to the needs of others. One of his "three wishes" was that "millions of dollars would go to the homeless."

The *Personality Inventory for Children* was administered to screen for developmental and emotional concerns, with Mrs. M. serving as informant. The resulting profile was considered to be valid and is consistent with that of youngsters who are often inattentive in class, do not complete homework assignments, and may require adult intervention to conform to stated limits. The PIC suggests that Pat may display limited frustration tolerance, which may be associated with temper tantrums or difficulties in peer relationships.

Other elevations on the PIC suggest that Pat's behavior at home may be characterized by resistance to requests from adults and a tendency to blame others for current problems. Implementation of a structured home discipline routine is likely to be helpful in reducing some of these noncompliant behaviors.

Educational Evaluation

Pat was evaluated by Dr. T., educational specialist. Pat was described by Dr. T. as a bright, articulate, pleasant child who fidgeted often in his seat and went from sitting to standing to kneeling. He had difficulty with longer explanations and would ask for questions to be repeated, especially in multistep questioning.

Test Results

Woodcock-Johnson Psychoeducational Battery

Subtest	Grade Score	Age Score	Percentile	Standard Score
Reading	2.4	7.7	53	101
Mathematics	1.4	6.8	14	84
Written Language	2.0	7.6	53	101
Knowledge	4.5	9.9	95	125

VMI—Revised

Age Equivalent: 7 years, 2 months
Standard Score: 96
Percentile: 39

These results demonstrate significant discrepancy in academic achievement when compared to ability testing on the WISC-R. Pat demonstrates a great strength in his acquired fund of knowledge and information in the areas of science, social studies, and humanities. Scores on the VMI-R indicate a slight weakness in visual motor integration. This could result in Pat having difficulties in copying from the board and drawing designs and patterns.

Weaknesses were noted in the area of math calculations, where Pat made errors of detail in calculations and answered problems rather impulsively. His reading skills show basic sight-word strength with weaker performance in passage comprehension.

Diagnostic Impression

Our impression of Pat is that of a youngster who has a learning disability with attention problems serving as a compounding factor to this underlying issue.

The psychological evaluation showed Pat to be a boy of high-average intellectual abilities who is not achieving at a level commensurate with his intellectual abilities on individual academic testing. Testing today revealed the presence of a specific learning disability in the area of math. Observation today also suggests that mild to moderate difficulties with attention and hyperactivity are also likely to affect Pat's behavior in the classroom and his peer relationships.

On the audiological evaluation, Pat's score on the screening test for standard auditory processing was well below the norm for a youngster of his age. Some sound discrimination issues were evident, along with multiple errors being made. Further workup in this regard would be appropriate.

Recommendations

1. Pat would also benefit from self-questioning techniques. Pat needs to develop an internal language of covert speech. He should be taught to answer the questions: "What is the problem? What am I supposed to do? What is my plan? How can I go about doing it? Am I using my plan? How did I do?" Pat has difficulty in organizing his material and behavior, and covert speech skills would be helpful.

2. Pat needs much drill and practice in basic math calculations. Review and overlearning would be important. He may enjoy learning facts in a rap music format. Contact Dr. T. for ordering information.

3. Pat will respond to brief activities containing variety. Worksheets should be divided into manageable chunks. Gradually increasing workloads should be presented.

4. The use of color cues would be helpful in helping Pat focus his attention. When teaching words, one should highlight in color the word parts for his added attention.

5. Follow-up audiological evaluation, especially in regard to central auditory processing, is recommended.

6. The multidisciplinary team at Pat's school should meet to discuss the results of Pat's testing and his general school performance. Placement in the LD resource classroom should be considered.

7. We concur with the continuation of a psychostimulant medication trial and feel that when medication is reinstituted Ritalin might be an appropriate alternative to Cylert at this point, especially in consideration of Pat's less-than-optimal response to Cylert.

8. Family counseling to help institute behavioral intervention at home may be useful.

9. All attempts should be made to continue providing enrichment opportunities that encourage general knowledge and motivation for learning. Taped books would be helpful for introducing a greater selection of information.

A follow-up visit with Dr. C. will be scheduled for about two months from now to review this report and discuss any further recommendations as necessary.

SAMPLE REPORT 2

Multidisciplinary Team Evaluation

Case: Ben F.

DOB: 4/18/78

Ben's parents are concerned because Ben has difficulty getting schoolwork done and paying attention in his classroom. They feel he takes little pride in his schoolwork and he needs help with self-discipline. The school has recommended retaining him, which his mother has agreed to do.

When he was in kindergarten, the *Iowa Test of Basic Skills* was administered, and Ben was felt at that time to be gifted. During the first grade, his Iowa scores fell to the 67th percentile, and he started to receive help in Chapter One with math.

Ben "hates" school, according to his mother. He doesn't bring work home from school and on one or two occasions, he has signed his mother's name to notes in order to get out of doing assignments.

Ben's gross motor skills are noted to be excellent. It is only in the area of academics that he has particular difficulty. He is felt to be a well-behaved child; however, his parents feel he is overactive. He can be unpredictable, impulsive, and difficult to satisfy.

On the *Diagnostic Interview for Children and Adolescents* from the Washington University School of Medicine, Ben scored positive on 9 of the 14 questions asked, meeting the criteria for attention-deficit/hyperactivity disorder. No other significant behavior problems were noted.

His parents view him rather positively and describe him as being a very affectionate, sympathetic, popular, and outgoing youngster, who confides in others easily and stands up for himself when necessary.

Background Information

Mrs. F. was happy when she became pregnant with Ben at the age of 20, and her pregnancy was unremarkable. Ben was born weighing 7 pounds, 12 1/2 ounces without any significant neonatal problems.

Ben sat without help and crawled by the age of six months and walked by the age of one year. He spoke his first words by the age of 12 months and was able to speak clearly enough that strangers could understand by the age of 18 months.

For the first several years of life he was "almost constantly on antibiotics." He had ear infections about two to three times a year up until the age of three and once or twice a year ever since. His mother noted that he has an allergy to milk and that he has been on a milk-free diet for the past several years.

Ben's parents have been divorced for the last three years. Both parents are college graduates. Ben lives with his mother and stepfather, who have been married for one year. Ben has a sister age 2 months.

School Information

Ben's teachers in the fourth grade note that he shows a lot of enthusiasm and he is motivated easily. He has difficulty staying on task and he has a short attention span compared with other fourth graders. His teachers point to problems with organizational skills and the fact that he tends to rush through his work. He appears to be satisfied with average or below average performance, and his maturity level seems below that of other fourth graders. His teachers would like to see him develop a stronger self-image and more self-discipline. They would also like to see Ben act in a more age-appropriate manner with his peers. He is described as having extreme trouble with concentration in large groups of children, and in response, he tends to annoy and bother other children. His teachers feel he doesn't seem to care about making mistakes, and they point out that he frequently tries to find fault with all of his work.

Clinical Evaluation

Ben separated easily from his mother for the physical assessment with Dr. P., M.D. His height was 53 inches and his weight was 71 pounds. Physical examination did not reveal any significant dysmorphic features or any significant abnormalities. The neurological examination did not reveal any focal or lateralizing findings. Deep tendon reflexes were equal and adequate bilaterally.

Ben underwent the *Neurodevelopmental Assessment for School-Age Children* (Levine). He was able to track horizontally and vertically without any difficulty; no difficulty with midline transitions, nystagmus, or strabismus were noted. He had some difficulty with maintaining a fixed motor stance, in that he had slight spooning of his outstretched arms with mild motoric impersistence. No significant choreiform movements were noted and he was easily able to maintain his stance. No significant synkinesis or elbow deviations were noted when Ben performed rapid alternating movements of his forearm. He was easily able to imitate finger movements (propriokinesthetic functioning). Ben had a good sense of laterality and was able to cross command on himself as well as the examiner without difficulty. He was right dominant in his eye, hand, and foot.

As far as temporal, sequential organizational skills were concerned, Ben had difficulty in repeating more than five digits forward, as well as in sequencing more than five objects in a row. These results indicate relative difficulty for him as compared to his peers. Ben also had difficulty in deciphering the names of the days of the week written backwards. He performed with brief hesitations in his responses as well as false starts when questioned in regard to the months of the year.

Ben's performance on the Auditory Language Function section was marred by his impulsivity, which tended to increase in highly verbal situations. When the examiner slowed down, made good eye contact with Ben, and gave him cues to follow, his performance improved markedly.

Ben presented as a child with good self-esteem through the course of the neurodevelopmental assessment. With the exception of poor visual and auditory sequencing, his overall performance was appropriate if somewhat impulsive. Impulsivity did not interfere significantly, especially when accommodations were made to suit his style. He was occasionally overactive. He was also fidgety. No yawning or stretching was noted. He tended to sustain his behavior over time and monitored well through the assessment. He was rather flexible and easily able to direct his attention to new tasks, and he never asked when the examination would be finished.

Ben adapted well to the examination, becoming immediately engaged. He was very cooperative and easily accepted directions. He did not exhibit any significant anxiety through the course of the assessment. His demeanor was consistently friendly, and his rare irritation was appropriate. His affective range was varied, and he was communicatively spontaneous through the course of the assessment. Vision evaluation was normal.

Educational Evaluation

Ben was evaluated by S.G., Ph.D., educational specialist. He was willing to work hard on the tasks presented but appeared somewhat anxious about his academic skills. He stated, "I hope you find out what is wrong with me." Dr. G. believes that today's test results provide a fair representation of his present academic functioning.

Test Results

Woodcock-Johnson Psychoeducational Battery

Subtest	Grade Score	Age Score	Percentile	Standard Score
Reading	4.5	9.9	42	97
Mathematics	5.6	11.0	72	109
Written Language	4.9	10.0	50	100
Knowledge	5.6	10.1	170	108
Skills	3.9	9.1	27	91

Wide Range Achievement Test

Subtest	Standard Score	Percentile	Grade Equivalent
Reading	87	19	3B
Spelling	100	50	5B
Arithmetic	99	47	4E

Development Test of Visual Motor Integration
Age Equivalent: 7 years, 3 months
Percentile: 13
Standard Score: 7

These results indicate that Ben is functioning at average to slightly below average levels in academic tasks. His reading ability and structural range are at the middle of the fourth-grade level, with strengths demonstrated in visual identification and gestalt functioning. Strengths were also evident in mathematics application and science understanding. The overall skills cluster scores demonstrate that Ben's basic skill ability in academic tasks is below average. This indicates an area of possible remediation and could prove to be an area of continual difficulty if these needs are not addressed.

Psychological Evaluation

Ben was evaluated by Dr. M., clinical psychologist. Assessment procedures utilized included a record review, the WISC-R, and the *Personality Inventory for Children—Revised*. In his working style, Ben responded quickly and efficiently for the most part. On math performance problems, his quick response style illustrated that he did not reflect on the problem before answering.

Ben was occasionally fidgety but was not overactive. He showed an acceptable tolerance for frustration and was challenged by difficult problems. The results of today's evaluation were considered to be a valid estimate of Ben's current abilities.

Test Results

Wechsler Intelligence Scale for Children—R

Verbal Tests	Standard Score
Information	10
Similarities	9
Arithmetic	10
Vocabulary	9
Comprehension	11
Digit Span	(10)

Performance Tests	
Picture Completion	11
Picture Arrangement	11
Block Design	12
Object Assembly	12
Coding	9

Verbal IQ	98 ± 7
Performance IQ	106 ± 8
Full-Scale IQ	102 ± 5

On the *Wechsler Intelligence Scale for Children—Revised,* Ben obtained a full-scale IQ score of 102 (90 percent confidence), which falls within the average range. This score was based on a verbal IQ score of 98 and a performance IQ score of 106, both also within the average range.

Overall, Ben's performance placed him at the 55th percentile when compared to his age peers. Ben's test profile showed relatively even performance with little inter- or intra-subtest scatter. A comparison of individual subtests showed no significant strengths or weaknesses. An analysis of factor scores comparing Ben's performance on subtests measuring verbal/perceptual skills, perceptual/organizational skills, and freedom from distractibility was performed, with no significant differences shown.

In summary, the results of the WISC-R showed Ben to be a boy of average intellectual abilities, with no relative processing weaknesses in either verbal or perceptual areas that could interfere with his academic performance.

Ben's mother was asked to complete the 280-item version of the *Personality Inventory for Children—Revised,* which is a further screen for attentional, behavioral, and emotional concerns. Her responses on the PIC appeared to accurately reflect her son's adjustment and not to exaggerate or minimize problems. Review of the factor scales on the PIC revealed greater than average concern, although not in the clinical range, regarding Ben's self-control and undisciplined behavior.

This suggested that Ben is a youngster who will have greater than average difficulty in controlling his impulses and monitoring his own performance on school-related tasks. Ben's profile was not elevated on a hyperactivity scale. This profile is often elevated with children who have difficulties in the classroom associated with impulsivity, distractibility, and restlessness. No other emotional or behavioral concerns were suggested by Ben's PIC profile. School achievement difficulties were shown.

Audiological Evaluation

Impedence audiometry revealed normal middle ear pressure bilaterally, with normal compliance recorded. Acoustic reflexes were screened at 100 dB HL. With either ear stimulated, contralateral and ipsilateral acoustic reflexes were absent at all test frequencies.

In summary, the audiological data appear consistent with normal hearing sensitivity; however, middle ear function is questioned.

Diagnostic Impression

Our impression of Ben today is that of a 10-year-old boy who presents with attentional problems in the classroom and whose teachers perceive that his immaturity warrants retaining him in the fourth grade for the coming academic year.

Ben's physical and neurological examinations were within normal limits today. Audiological assessment was also within normal limits, although some concerns about middle ear functioning were noted. He was noted to be a well-adjusted, neatly groomed youngster who had good self-esteem and a very realistic approach to the difficulties that he is encountering. The results of the psychological evaluation suggested that Ben is a boy of average intellectual potential. Academic skills generally fell within the average range. No evidence of processing problems in either verbal or perceptual areas were suggested by the WISC-R. No significant attentional problems were shown on a one-on-one basis, either through the psychological assessment or through the neurodevelopmental assessment, although some degree of impulsivity was noted. Ben's history is positive for attentional problems in the classroom.

The results of the *Personality Inventory for Children* supported greater than average difficulties with self-control, self-discipline, and other school achievement measures. No other indicators of significant emotional behavioral disturbances were suggested by the PIC, Ben's history, or the evaluation performed today.

Ben did have difficulty with overall organizational skills, memory skills, and attention, as noted. By history, both from his parents and from his teachers, he meets the criteria of having attention-deficit/hyperactivity disorder, and these findings were discussed with parents at the conclusion of today's visit.

Recommendations

1. In regard to Ben's attentional problems, we do not feel that Ben is currently a candidate for retention. We feel, indeed, that classroom accommodations should be made to suit his particular style, and we hope to emphasize that during the course of this report. Dr. P. will follow up in about three months, at which time Ben's progress will be reviewed and further recommendations will be made as necessary.

2. Although Ben does not appear to qualify for special education services through his school, classroom accommodations should be made as noted. Because of his difficulty in self-monitoring, Ben will respond best to a very rich schedule of reinforcement and consequences to maintain his on-task behaviors. A token system may be useful initially. In such a system, his teacher will monitor his on- and off-task behavior on a regular basis. Tokens are given for on-task behaviors and can be redeemed for a variety of rewards. His teacher will also give tokens for work completed in the classroom. Ben could be taught to take over responsibility for monitoring by rating his attention every five minutes. (An egg timer could be used for such timing.)

3. In the fall, at the time of follow-up, Ben's classroom attention will be rated by his teacher using the *Conners' Teacher Rating Scale*. At that time, should his attentional problems still be of concern, the prescribing of psychostimulant medications would be considered.

4. Ben will be seen by Dr. G. at that time for a further evaluation of possible use of medication.

5. Ben responds well to immediate feedback and, therefore, a computer could be a very effective teaching tool in reinforcing basic math and reading skills.

6. Pairing Ben with a same-age peer on special classroom projects can also be used as a reward for school assignment completion. This will also help in developing Ben's social skills and sensitivity to interpersonal cues.

SAMPLE REPORT 3

Psychoeducational Evaluation

Case: HC

DOB: 2/25/87

Reason for Referral

HC was referred by her parents and teachers at Lincoln School for a complete evaluation of her strengths and weaknesses as a learner.

Background Information

Mrs. C. completed the *ANSER Parent Questionnaire* and shared the following information. HC is the result of a 38-week pregnancy and a difficult Cesarean delivery, and weighed 5 pounds 1 ounce at birth. HC had some difficulty sucking during the first six weeks and was supplemented with formula while breast feeding. HC has a history of ear infections between 4 months and 3 years and has some difficulty with food and other allergies. Functionally, Mrs. C. reports that HC had feeding difficulties throughout her early development and was unwilling to try new foods. Recently, she reports stomachaches, trouble falling asleep, and some difficulty in being comforted or consoled. Her mother states that there is a background of shyness with strangers and bashfulness with new children.

Early developmental milestones were normal. Family history includes the mother having difficulty learning to read and some history of the grandfather having similar difficulties. HC currently resides with her parents. Her father is a professional basketball player, and the family is often able to accompany him to different training camps and games throughout the school year. HC has a younger brother, age 3.

Mrs. C. shares that HC is at times poorly coordinated, can become confused, forgets words and often mispronounces them. In the area of attention and activity, Mrs. C. found seven areas of concern for HC on the *Levine Selective Attention Scale* and noted that HC is moody, cries easily, and often complains of pains in her arms or legs. Associated strengths are that she is an affectionate girl who stands up for herself when necessary. In her mother's words, HC is a child who, when she is happy, can walk into a room and light it up. Mrs. C sees HC's emotional highs and lows as being intense, and the girl has difficulty with sleep patterns, often waking up in the middle of the night with night terrors.

182

Behavioral Observation

HC joined both examiners readily, but she was shy initially. She was well groomed, although she had a runny nose. She was very cooperative, but very little smiling was noted. Overall, she appeared to have fairly flat affect. Throughout testing both examiners noted creativity, with good planning at first, and then a breakdown of skills as she worked longer. Expressive language was age appropriate and she had legible printing.

<u>Evaluation Procedures</u>
ANSER Parent Questionnaire
Parent Interview
WPPSI-R
Woodcock-Johnson Psychoeducational Battery—Revised, Tests of Achievement
Peabody Picture Vocabulary Test
Developmental Test of Visual Motor Integration
KABC Achievement Subtests
Token Test for Children

Evaluation Results

Kaufman Assessment Battery for Children

Achievement Subtest	Standard Score +/- Band of Error 90% Confidence
Faces and Places	103 ± 11
Arithmetic	99 ± 8
Riddles	110 ± 10
Reading/Decoding	101 ± 6
Overall Achievement	103 ± 5

Developmental Test of Visual Motor Integration—Revised

Age Equivalent	4 years, 10 months
Standard Score	84
Percentile	14

WPPSI-R

Performance IQ	100
Verbal IQ	107
Full-Scale IQ	103

Subtests

Object Assembly	14
Geometric Design	9
Mazes	9
Block Design	6
Picture Completion	12
Animal Pegs	19
Information	11
Comprehension	10
Arithmetic	10
Vocabulary	11
Similarities	14
Sentences	11

Peabody Picture Vocabulary Test—Revised

Standard Score: 97
Percentile: 42
Age Equivalent: 5 years, 7 months
Stanine: 5

Token Task for Children

Part 1:   501
Part 2:   503
Part 3:   504
Part 4:   508
Part 5:   507
Overall Score: Average Performance

Woodcock-Johnson Psychoeducational Battery—Revised
Tests of Achievement

	Age Score	Grade Score	Standard Score	%ile
Letter-Word Identification	5.11	K.7	98	45
Passage Comprehension	5.6	K.0	88	21
Calculation	4.11	K.0	88	21
Applied Problems	5.9	K.5	99	47
Dictation	6.4	1.1	110	75
Science	7.2	1.9	121	92
Social Studies	7.5	1.9	120	90
Humanities	6.8	1.3	108	70
Broad Reading			93	32
Broad Mathematics			92	33
Broad Knowledge			114	82
Skills			102	57

Interpretation of Test Results

The results of today's psychoeducational evaluation on the WPPSI-R reveal an average IQ with no significant difference between the performance and verbal scores. Throughout testing, HC needed frequent breaks and was often looking out the window. She remained in her seat, but appeared to be a daydreamer and impulsive. Often she hurried on geometrical designs. Good planning was noted initially, but planning broke down as she worked over a longer period of time. She often answered quickly, but with incomplete information. Throughout testing, HC seemed to be involved in some tasks and uninterested in others, but she remained seated and on task. Language appeared age appropriate. Both examiners noted excellent visual discrimination. At times her drawing and copying were affected by her hurried approach. Performance subtest scores, with the exception of Animal Pegs and Object Assembly, were affected by concentration. Her concentration for nonverbal tasks seemed to "flicker in and out." Overall reasoning skills were excellent. However, she does not seem to try harder when the task is difficult.

On the KABC, the strongest area was Riddles. HC enjoyed this section and also liked the Animal Peg section on the WPPSI-R. On the WPPSI-R, arithmetic was her weakest subtest. She often impulsively counted without getting all information and left out numbers in counting.

The Token Test for Children, which uses visual and motor responses, was far more interesting for her, and she was able to perform in an average range on that test.

184

Throughout academic testing, she was very fidgety and touched everything. Difficulty with listening was noted at times, and HC appeared to be an impulsive test-taker. She was pleasant to work with and demonstrated strong expressive skills. HC is right-handed but left-eyed, and had some difficulty due to weak sequencing skills.

On the *Woodcock-Johnson* battery, her strongest area was general information and dictation, with weaker areas in recall of letters and number identification.

Summary and Recommendations

HC is a 5-year-old girl who was referred for psychoeducational evaluation by her parents and her school due to concerns about her ability to attend to tasks and to function well in the academic environment. Current standardized intelligence tests indicate that HC's verbal and visual perceptual skills are in the average range of functioning. Based on educational testing, HC's expressive and receptive language functioning appears to be age appropriate. Strengths were demonstrated in the area of visual gestalt, overall general knowledge, long-term memory, and information analysis. Weaknesses were demonstrated in the areas of short-term memory, block design (which incorporates visual motor integration), impulsivity, and concentration for tasks as they become more complex.

The following recommendations are made to HC's parents and teachers:

1. HC appears to perform better in a classroom environment that is characterized by brief, varying lessons and short assignments, with frequent opportunities for praise and reinforcement. She responds well to incentives and behavior modification.

2. Whenever possible, HC should be seated near the teacher and away from distractors such as windows, interesting centers in the room, and talkative classmates.

3. It is recommended that her parents and the school staff make a special effort to communicate in developing a positive educational environment and program for HC. Tutoring this summer should be helpful, and consistent cooperation between home and school is highly advisable.

4. HC's parents should consider exploring with a physician the advantages and disadvantages of a trial of an appropriate medication, such as Ritalin. Symptoms present in the evaluation indicate undifferentiated attention deficit disorder.

5. HC's approach to her work is shaped by the attention deficit and by her weakness in the overall area of sequencing and details. The attention deficit influences her performance in terms of impulsivity and giving up.

6. Academic skills are mixed. Phonic and word attack skills for reading are below average. Spelling is accurate using a sight-word approach. As might be expected with impulsivity, the poor auditory processing pattern that HC exhibited is caused by not listening carefully to the sounds of words she is trying to spell. In reading, HC is depending on sight vocabulary and tries to guess at unknown words from the initial letters and overall configuration of the word. She will need help in developing reading skills to bridge some of her gaps in decoding and sight vocabulary. In tutoring this summer, an emphasis on decoding and using visual skills will be important.

7. Teachers should avoid timed tests. If timed tests are required, HC would do better to take them at home or alone, trying to beat her own past record rather than competing with her classmates.

8. HC benefits from observing others before attempting new tasks. She does model well and needs to be able to visually review tasks before attempting them.

9. HC's parents may be interested in a social-skills program that is available through the center, both during the school year and in the summer. It may help HC develop some skills in attention and concentration, reduce her impulsivity, and help her learn how to cooperate with friends in a group situation.

10. It is recommended that HC's parents have the opportunity to acquire information regarding attention deficit disorder. A video is available here for parents to view. A list of support groups within the area has been given to her parents. It is important for parents to understand more about attention deficit disorder and to learn behavior management techniques.

SAMPLE REPORT 4

Educational Evaluation

Case: JD

DOB: 4/22/79

Educational Evaluation and Review

This evaluation included the psychological evaluation sent by San Diego Unified School District, which included the following tests: *Wechsler Intelligence Scale for Children—Revised, Woodcock-Johnson Psychoeducational Battery, Bender Visual Motor Gestalt Test, Beery Visual Motor Integration Test, Bristol Social Adjustment Guide, Devereux Child Behavior Rating Scale, Incomplete Sentences, Human Figures Drawings, Structured Interview, the Kinetic-Family Drawing,* and the *Piers-Harris Children's Self-Concept Scale.* Mrs. D. made these materials available for review by the educational diagnostician.

JD is currently a fourth grader at Desert Flower Elementary School. Information on his classroom behavior and achievement was received from RL, his current teacher. Mr. L. completed the *ANSER School Questionnaire* and described JD's difficulties as resulting from a lack of concentration, difficulty in initiating work, and often talking out in class. Mr. L. believes JD's strengths are that he is good-natured, he does not hold grudges, he reads well, and he responds to praise. Mr. L. asked for help in improving JD's concentration and for ideas to get JD to start and finish schoolwork.

In an interview prior to today's testing, Mrs. D. was able to give background information regarding JD's school history. JD has been attending Desert Flower Elementary School since the second grade. He has received help in a special reading program for the past two years. Mrs. D. has been concerned with JD's behavior in that teachers continually report he is constantly talking and disrupting other students. In addition, she has been very concerned about his poor handwriting skills and feels that his work is often illegible. In 1987, he was referred to an occupational therapist who found that he had mild motor problems and difficulties with motor control; however, under the school program guidelines, they were not severe enough to make JD eligible for therapy. Further evaluations took place in the San Diego School District and, since that date, JD has been receiving special education resource help for his written language difficulties. Currently, JD is averaging failing grades in school, with an F in both math and spelling. He is currently passing health and science. Mrs. D. and Mr. L. report that, as of late, JD is giving up and feels defeated before he even tries. Mom's interpretation of JD is that he "just can't help it." She believes something interferes with his learning, and she feels it has to do with his attention. She feels JD is frustrated and just won't try any more.

Following today's evaluation, JD is scheduled for an appointment with a developmental pediatrician. Today's evaluation will include a review of the school district report and additional testing done today. Instruments used were the *Developmental Test of Visual Motor Integration, and Woodcock-Johnson Psychoeducational Battery,* and the *Williamson Sentence Completion Test.* In addition, JD was observed in a play situation and then responded to a short dictation test. Vision and hearing screenings done by a nurse were normal. I believe these results give an accurate assessment of JD's present academic functioning.

Test Results

Woodcock-Johnson Psychoeducational Battery, Form B

	Grade Score	Age Score	Percentile	Standard Score
Reading	5.1	10.8	72	109
Mathematics	4.1	9.5	36	95
Written Language	4.4	9.5	50	100
Knowledge	6.7	12.3	93	122

Development Test of Visual Motor Integration

VMI Raw Score: 14
VMI Age Equivalent: 7 years, 3 months
Percentile: 23
Standard Score: 7

These results indicate that JD is functioning at an average level of achievement. Scores range from a weakness in math at the 36th percentile to a high in general knowledge of 93 percent. JD demonstrated difficulties in the area of math application. He has mastered the rote repetition of basic facts, but the integration of this information is very difficult for him. He had trouble concentrating on details within word story problems. Strengths for JD were in the area of reading, with strong sight-word identification (configuration) skills. He demonstrated above average ability in comprehension and word attack analysis. Scores on the dictation and proofing subtests of the *Woodcock-Johnson* have improved since last year and demonstrate the benefit of the one-to-one and small-group instruction JD has received in this area. Visual motor integration tasks remain two to three years delayed and account for the great difficulty that JD is having in copying from the board and completing written assignments. Overall strengths in science, social studies, and humanities show his strong verbal expression and ability to access his acquired fund of knowledge. During testing, he wiggled about a great deal, and daydreamed. In the mathematics section, he impulsively answered questions with no regard to computational details such as signs, carrying, and regrouping activities.

On the *Williamson Sentence Completion Test,* JD performed within normal limits with no unusual requests or wishes. He showed a concern about overeating sweets and a fear of heights. He did not demonstrate depression or any unusual patterns of self-concept. However, it should be noted that in the general knowledge section of the *Woodcock-Johnson,* JD put a question mark on the end of each of his answers. For example:

Q: "Who wrote *Green Eggs and Ham?*"
JD's answer: "Dr. Seuss?"

Q: "What is H_2O?"
JD's answer: "Water?"

In addition, JD had trouble concentrating when there was noise outside the room, and he stopped periodically to ask, "What's going on out there?" and "Did you hear that noise?"

Interpretation of Test Results from Desert Flower School

In the intellectual area of the WISC-R, JD appears to be functioning in the high average range in verbal intelligence and the average range in performance. Of note were difficulties with the coding subtest and extremely low scores in block design. Block design is one standard deviation below the population means. JD demonstrated great difficulty in reproducing patterns and designs. In addition and supportive of these results were scores on the VMI, where JD earned an age equivalent of 5 years, 1 month, and an almost equal score on the Bender, where his developmental age was 5 years, 5 months. Errors on both tests demonstrated that JD had difficulty with distortion, integration, and rotation, which would result in difficulty in copying and reproducing designs.

Academic performance, as measured by the Woodcock-Johnson, has improved since previous testing, although math scores have now dropped lower than what they were previously. At the time of testing a year ago, the total math score was at the 72nd percentile by age and considered to be above average. He now scores in the 36th percentile, which gives him an average standard score of 95. Results on the *Devereux Child Behavior Scale* completed by JD's parents revealed significant factors above the mean in distractibility, coordination, messiness, and unresponsiveness to stimulation. Factors were similar on the *Bristol Social Adjustment Guide*, which was filled out by his second-grade teacher, Mrs. M. At that point, Mrs. M. distinguished the following characteristics: inattentive, distractible, hyperactive, lacking the confidence to try anything different or difficult. All other measures of social and emotional adjustment were unremarkable.

Reactions appeared normal with the exception of a lack of concentration on the visual motor tasks. Although an occupational therapist felt that an intervention program would be helpful, JD's case was not severe enough to warrant attention.

Recommendations for the classroom included learning in small-group situations, reducing written assignments, and helping JD organize his materials and schedule. It was also stated that because he is better at auditory than visual learning, spelling out loud would be helpful for his work.

Summary and Recommendations

JD is a bright young boy who exhibits difficulty with visual motor integration, distractibility, and impulsivity. Both JD's parents and his teachers report that he tends to "tune out" as work gets difficult, resorting to quickly finishing a page or guessing to complete the task, and this behavior was observed during individual testing today as well.

Today's testing suggests that JD's behavior should be further evaluated by Dr. L. for the possible presence of an attention deficit disorder. In addition to signs of inattention, current testing suggests some weakness in abstract reasoning, concept formation, and similar higher-order cognitive skills. Hence, despite his superior verbal skills, JD is having some difficulty understanding and applying abstract ideas. At this stage of his educational career, these difficulties may be most evident in his understanding of mathematics concepts. JD's problems are subtle but, nonetheless, quite real and are consistent with his parents' observations of his difficulties.

The following approaches might be explored to support JD:

1. The further exploration of this material with Dr. L. Dr. L. has stated she would like to share the possible advantages and disadvantages of a trial of an appropriate pharmacological approach, such as Ritalin.

2. The design of an accommodation plan in the classroom to meet JD's particular needs.

3. Additional ideas to build visual motor integration skills. Even though JD is not eligible for services, the school therapist may suggest to Mrs. D. some ideas for home therapy that might build JD's self-confidence in pursuing visual motor tasks.

4. Because handwriting is an extremely difficult task that may interfere with his educational performance, JD's knowledge of subject matter could be better assessed using methods requiring limited production of written language. A multiple-choice response format or oral testing is preferable to short-answer or essay formats.

5. Encourage JD to develop written language abilities using keyboarding skills. The generation of language does not appear to be JD's difficulty; therefore, the use of assistive devices like a word processor is strongly advised to assist in the production of written language.

6. A hand-held spelling dictionary may be helpful for JD, and it may also help to have someone proofread his written papers before he hands them in.

Following today's evaluation, Mrs. D. was given the *ACTeRS Form* and the *Conners' Teacher Rating Scale* to give to JD's teachers in order to provide Dr. L. with information from the classroom teachers.

SAMPLE REPORT 5

Educational Evaluation

Case: MM

DOB: 10/10/72

Reason for Referral

MM was referred to Dr. S. for continued evaluation of her educational strengths and weaknesses. MM was recently diagnosed as having attention deficit disorder by Dr. A. The parents were seeking additional input and information regarding MM's concentration and attention difficulties.

Background Information

MM graduated from Smith Academy in San Jose and is presently a sophomore at the University of Arizona. She qualified for placement in a learning disabilities program and, during her first year at school, received help from the SALT (Learning Disability) Program. Currently she is not receiving SALT services but is seeing a private tutor twice a week. She is also on psychostimulant medication, which she is taking under the supervision of Dr. A.

Evaluation Procedures

Woodcock-Johnson Psychoeducational Battery—Revised, Form A Tests of Achievement
Kagan Matching Figures Test
Williamson Sentence Completion Test
Ayres Test of Visual Pursuit
Finger Sequencing

Evaluation Results

Ayres Test of Visual Pursuit: 90 to 100 degree marking. MM was able to follow an object to full horizontal and vertical ranges of movement. There was no jerkiness in eye pursuit movements and no difficulty crossing midline.

Woodcock-Johnson Psychoeducational Battery—Revised
Tests of Achievement

	Age Score	Grade Score	Standard Score	%ile
Letter-Word Identification	27	16.8	111	77
Passage Comprehension	22	14.2	104	61
Calculation	17.0	10.7	98	45
Applied Problems	14.6	9.4	91	28
Dictation	14.1	8.9	92	30
Writing Samples	20	12.9	100	50
Science	13.4	8.1	90	25
Social Studies	14.6	9.1	90	25
Humanities	18.6	12.4	99	45
Broad Reading			109	72
Broad Mathematics			94	34
Broad Written Language			89	23
Broad Knowledge			91	27
Skills			91	27

Kagan Matching Figures Test: Below normal

Finger Sequencing: MM was unable to touch the second, third, and fourth fingers in sequence with her eyes closed on several attempts, nor to repeat which fingers were touched.

Interpretation of Test Results

Educational testing on the *Woodcock-Johnson Tests of Achievement* demonstrate that MM is currently functioning above grade level in Letter-Word Identification and Passage Comprehension, and below grade level in the areas of Calculation, Application of Problems, Dictation, and Writing Samples. Particular strengths were noted in overall broad reading skills and sight word vocabulary. Additional strengths were noted in the area of humanities. Weakness was noted in the areas of Dictation, Calculation, and Recall of General Facts in Science and Social Studies. MM demonstrated difficulty in recalling basic facts, rote memorization, and information base. She appeared to have strong sight vocabulary and her reading comprehension using context clues was above average.

Disorganized visual motor planning difficulties were noted on *the Kagan Matching Figures Test.* MM has strong spatial abilities and underdeveloped sequencing skills. She has difficulty with spelling and often spells words according to their overall appearance rather than sounding them out sound-by-sound. Difficulties with short-term memory and impulsivity were also exhibited during testing.

Strengths for MM also lie in verbal reasoning skills and receptive language. Weaknesses were in attention to detail, following four-step directions, and memorization of rote material.

No emotional or psychological difficulties were noted in a personal interview or on the *Williamson Sentence Completion Test*. MM appears to have strong moral convictions, feels deeply about her difficulties with impulsivity and inattention, and appears to value her strong family relationships. She recognizes her limits and expresses concern that she can be tactless with friends and family members.

Summary and Recommendations

This evaluation found MM to be a young lady of average to below average academic abilities with particular strengths in verbal skills. Scores demonstrate a background history of difficulty with inattention, concentration, and impulsivity. Of particular note is MM's background history of poor recall of information for facts in the areas of science and social studies. It appears that she has many gaps in her background information due to her difficulty with inattention. MM and her parents report that at times she "tunes out" when work becomes difficult. Her instructors have reported that she appears to begin guessing in order to complete the task if she is not focused on the directions. This was observed today during individual testing. Current testing certainly documents that MM's behavior is consistent with the presence of attention deficit disorder which is associated with mild chronic neuropsychological dysfunction. For MM, this condition occurs without overt hyperactivity, although some tapping and fidgeting are noted. At times, she has greater than usual difficulty in following through on directions and concentrating on a task. When pressure increases, for example, during timed or individual testing, she states that she rushes through the test.

In addition to attention deficit disorder, current testing suggests some weaknesses in abstract reasoning and sequential skills. MM's problems are subtle yet quite real and are consistent with her own comments and her parents' observations of her difficulties. The introduction of a psychostimulant appears to have been most helpful for MM, and she is cognizant of its effect when she is taking it. It appears to offer her improvement in concentration and attention, and she also reports improvement in socialization skills. MM continues to need systematic instruction, abstract reasoning skills, and concept formation skills, with help in learning to observe similarities, and categorization. It is important that her tutor help her to appreciate and understand a variety of study skills which are geared to her particular strengths and weaknesses. Continued growth in these skills should help her organize her work and increase her visual motor planning. Work with a tutor is also necessary to fill gaps in MM's basic skills, and she needs to keep up-to-date in her educational efforts.

Additionally, MM should increase her work on computer applications. She would benefit from developing her written language skills, and the use of a word processor is highly recommended. MM has no difficulty with the generation of language, but she does have trouble with spelling, capitalization, and punctuation. Therefore, she needs to begin using a word processor to assist in production of written language.

When studying, MM needs to avoid rote memorization. Greater use of conceptual and highly visual pieces of information will help her recall. Color coding and highlighting material of high interest will also be important. MM may benefit from listening to taped books for book reports and for learning information. Audiotapes should be more interesting to her and help her focus her attention more than reading written material alone.

In addition, she will benefit from study groups in which she can talk about certain academic topics with other students in her class. Study groups should improve her retention due to her strong auditory skills.

Suggestions were given to MM today to help her stay on task in class; using techniques such as "Stop, take time to listen—Stop, take time to check" was also recommended. It is important that she place herself near the front of the room and get copies of other students' lecture notes. Review of these notes is crucial prior to testing situations.

In the future, MM needs to break assignments into segments and learn to organize her ideas sequentially. She will benefit from attending the ADD Adult Support Group in Tucson. Phone and contact information were relayed.

Continued management of the medication with Dr. A.'s expertise is important. We were able to discuss the dynamics of the medication and to talk about several other aspects of its use.

MM has many strengths in verbal expression, creativity, and the ability to visually interpret materials. It is important that she begin to use the possibilities her strengths offer her in conquering some of the academic difficulties she has been having.

SAMPLE REPORT 6

Educational Evaluation

Case: JG

DOB: 6/19/83

Reason for Referral

JG was referred to this examiner by Dr. D., family pediatrician. JG's parents have been concerned about reports from school that JG has difficulties with attention, concentration, and transferring written information.

Background Information

The *ANSER Parent Questionnaire* was completed by Mrs. G. and included the following information. JG was the result of a difficult 9-month pregnancy. Forceps were used in the last five minutes of delivery due to concerns about his heart rate. He weighed 7 pounds, 5 1/2 ounces at birth. Health problems have been nonsignificant. Parents do relate a history of colic, overactivity, temper tantrums, and difficulty in keeping to a schedule. Early developmental milestones were normal, with the exception of teachers reporting some behavior problems in kindergarten and nursery school. Both parents report a family history of some difficulties with hyperactivity and learning.

JG currently lives with his parents, who are both in good health. His father has some college education, and his mother is currently attending college to become a teacher. His parents report that, although they think JG is a bright child, he has difficulty staying on task and writing.

The *ANSER School Questionnaire* was completed by JG's teacher in the gifted program, Mrs. W. She reported that JG is bright but seems to be well behind what she would expect for someone with JG's aptitude. She sees JG as highly distractible and in constant motion, physically and mentally. She reports that he is very impulsive in his actions.

Behavioral Observation

JG joined this examiner readily. He was cooperative throughout testing and applied an appropriate level of effort to the materials. Wandering attention was noted throughout tasks. The present data are seen as an accurate reflection of his current functioning, but consideration should be given to his high level of inattention during sustained tasks when interpreting the results.

Evaluation Procedures

ANSER Parent Questionnaire
ANSER School Questionnaire
Parent Interview
Woodcock-Johnson Psychoeducational Battery—Revised, Tests of Achievement
Woodcock-Johnson Tests of Cognitive Ability
Detroit Test of Learning Aptitude (Partial)
Developmental Test of Visual Motor Integration
ACTeRS Checklist
Levine Selective Attention Profile
Williamson Sentence Completion Test
Kagan Matching Familiar Figures Test

Evaluation Results

Developmental Test of Visual Motor Integration—Revised

Age Equivalent: 11 years, 2 months
Standard Score: 111
Percentile: 77

Detroit Test of Learning Aptitude (Partial)

Subtest	Percentile	Standard Score
Object Sequences	75	12
Letter Sequences	37	9

Levine Selective Attention Profile: All scores were in the range of severe attention concerns.

ACTeRS Checklist

Attention	7	Difficulty—Attention	Severe
Hyperactivity	23	Difficulty—Hyperactivity	Severe
Social Skills	23	Difficulty—Social Skills	Mild
Oppositional	18	Difficulty—Oppositional	Moderate

Kagan Matching Familiar Figures Test: Below average

Woodcock-Johnson Psychoeducational Battery—Revised
Tests of Achievement

	Age Score	Grade Score	Standard Score	%ile
Letter-Word Identification	10.9	5.4	109	73
Passage Comprehension	13.8	8.3	127	96
Calculation	10.4	5.0	118	88
Applied Problems	13.11	8.7	136	99
Dictation	10.1	4.6	106	65
Writing Samples	10.4	5.1	109	72
Science	13.4	8.1	128	97
Social Studies	12.6	7.0	128	97
Humanities	10.2	4.8	105	64
Broad Reading			118	88
Broad Mathematics			132	98
Broad Written Language			108	69
Broad Knowledge			122	93
Skills			116	86

Woodcock-Johnson Tests of Cognitive Ability

	Age Score	Grade Score	Standard Score	%ile
Visual Processing				
Visual Matching	8.3	2.8	87	19
Cross Out	8.3	2.9	90	26
Short-Term Memory				
Numbers Reversed	10.7	5.3	109	72
Memory for Sentences	12.3	6.7	109	72
Memory for Words	11.1	6.6	108	70

Interpretation of Test Results

Behavioral ratings at school indicate extreme difficulties with inattention, impulsivity, and hyperactivity when JG is involved in academic tasks. Problems with attention were decreased in the one-to-one situation of this evaluation. The parents reported concerns of a similar nature, but not as severe as the teacher's assessment. As JG is an only child, it is not inconsistent that only mild impulsive/hyperactive problems are noted at home.

JG appears to be a youngster of superior intelligence with superior spatial reasoning skills and a high level of acquired knowledge. His current progress in academics has not kept pace with his intellectual skills, however. Generally his academic progress is at a high average level for his age in reading and mathematics reasoning. Eye-hand coordination is in the average range, and handwriting is marginal in quality. Written calculation is average, most likely the result of inhibited thinking while writing, which increases his withdrawal of attention and decreases learning.

On the *Woodcock-Johnson Tests of Cognitive Ability,* processing speed was well below average. It is felt that JG's distractibility caused the difficulty in processing recorded on this measure, whereas the task demand for increased attention on the Object Sequences on the DTLA resulted in normal performance. The Cross Out test on the WJR is a visual recognition task requiring sustained attention for three minutes. JG's performance is below average at the 26th percentile. His score on the Memory for Sentences subtest is in the high average range, indicating stronger short-term retention for oral material. The sequential processing demand in the Sentence Recall test does not negatively affect his performance.

JG's difficulty with sustained attention in class is likely to result from a difficulty in mental control with secondary hyperactivity, which interacts with the social and cognitive demands of the situation. Individual testing by this examiner and comments by the teacher show that JG's behavior is characterized by distractibility, impulsivity, and some oppositional behavior. It was reported by JG's parents and teacher that he may "space out" when work gets boring or involves many written tasks. At this point, he resorts to guessing in order to complete the task. This behavior was observed, together with signs of distress, such as fidgeting, impulsivity, and moving often in his seat.

Summary and Recommendations

JG is a bright 9-year-old boy who demonstrates significantly superior ability and is currently attending the gifted program in his elementary school. Difficulties in attention and concentration have been reported by his parents and by the classroom teacher. JG's behavior today indicated difficulty with impulsivity, attention to task, and completion of activities. In addition, below average skills were noted in processing speed, visual memory, and visual recognition tasks requiring sustained memory.

JG's variability in scores today is consistent with the educational profile of a child with attention deficit, and it is recommended that parents share this information with their physician for further assessment. Observations and achievement test results substantiate this need for further evaluation.

The following recommendations are made to JG's parents.

1. Attention focus is facilitated by a nondistracting environment and interesting presentations in an active environment. Direct eye contact and perhaps body contact (e.g., a finger touch on the hand or shoulder) may be used to assist JG. Asking JG questions rather than telling him information will keep his attention engaged. Examples: "What do you think makes the apple fall?" "What are the three things you put on the paper before you start?"

2. JG should be encouraged to restate information he is given. When instructions containing new information are given, it is helpful for JG to be required to actively participate while he's listening; for instance, by filling in a worksheet that coincides with the auditory instructions.

3. JG will learn best if information is presented both auditorially and visually, and whenever possible, if an active motor response is encouraged.

   Accurate multimodality rehearsal involves self-vocalization (softly restating the information to one's self), visualization (which may require drawing a diagram of the information or studying related pictures), and tactile-kinesthetic rehearsal (tracing, copying, or finger drawing on the hand).

   One study strategy that may be helpful is "Read, Cover, Recite, Check" (or RCRC): After several *readings*, *cover* the material and try to *say* it, then write it to *check* the accuracy and completeness of the memory.

4. In the future, the computer will be an excellent tool for JG. It can be extremely helpful for the practice of such things as math facts and should be used liberally for this purpose. Chunking and linking—connecting various pieces of new information through logic, intrinsic associations, pattern identification, pictures, or imposed mnemonic devices will involve JG in the active creative process of remembering. A computer-based course in memory strategies would be helpful. Also, JG may have more success recalling basic math facts using a rap melody, such as *Multiplication and Division Rap*, which is available through a teacher's supply outlet.

5. Teach JG to become a list maker. Create a short list of daily activities and have him cross off each item as he completes it.

6. JG's parents were given a videotape to view: *Why Won't My Child Pay Attention?* In addition, they were given reading materials dealing with the topics of learning and attention.

SAMPLE REPORT 7

Educational Evaluation

Case: MB

DOB: 5/12/84

Reason for Referral

MB was referred for further educational evaluation following a diagnosis of ADHD by a psychiatrist several years ago. MB currently attends St. Luke Parochial School where she is a third grader.

Background Information

The *ANSER Parent Questionnaire* was completed by Mrs. B. She shared that MB is the result of an 8½-month pregnancy and weighed 8 pounds, 12 ounces at birth. MB has a history of some difficulty with ear infections between 19 months and 3 years. Early developmental milestones were normal with the exception of gross motor tasks, which were somewhat delayed. Parents noticed that when she was a toddler, MB would often fall and not protect herself by putting her arms out.

Currently food allergies to both milk and sugar have been noted. Mrs. B. also reports that MB is a very heavy sleeper who often has difficulty in being comforted or consoled. She can be irritable at times and does have extreme reactions to noise or sudden movements. It is also noted that MB has difficulty keeping to a schedule.

MB attended preschool and nursery school, where teachers reported some difficulty with selective hearing. She was retained in kindergarten at age 5.

MB currently lives with her parents and older sister, age 16. Her parents are high school graduates with advanced education and are in good health.

Her parents see MB as a creative child with many interests who often notices things that no one else does. They feel that she gets "burned out" too easily when expected to concentrate and that she is able to remember minor details better than most people can. They feel she is never bored, but is very restless and can be a poor listener. When asked to sit still and concentrate, they find she is fidgety and prefers being active.

The *ANSER School Questionnaire* was completed by MB's classroom teacher, Ms. T. She reports that MB is very active and feels that MB's present strengths are in mathematics. At times MB seems to know information, Ms. T. reports, but she doesn't always seem to be able to follow through. Ms. T. feels that MB is not as organized and is not able to follow directions quite as well as her classmates. Her teacher reports that positive reinforcement does not seem to make much difference with MB. She feels that MB has great difficulty performing tasks. Behavior is generally off-task.

MB was evaluated by Dr. X. at Children's Hospital in the fall of 1989. In his report, he points out significant difficulties with attention and is concerned about MB's lack of inhibition and her distractibility. On the *Wechsler Preschool Primary Test of Intelligence*, MB's verbal IQ was 126, performance IQ was 111, and full-scale IQ was 121. *Wide Range Achievement Test* results show a 97 standard score in reading, 103 score in spelling, and 85 in arithmetic. Although Dr. X. did not identify a learning disability, he felt that MB would definitely be an inefficient learner in a regular classroom, given her level of distractibility and overall attentional problems.

Evaluation Procedures

Review of previous psychometric summary
Review of *ANSER Parent Questionnaire* and *ANSER School Questionnaire*
Parent Interview
Woodcock-Johnson Psychoeducational Battery—Revised Tests of Achievement
Woodcock-Johnson Test of Cognitive Ability
Peabody Picture Vocabulary Test—Revised
Developmental Test of Visual Motor Integration

Evaluation Results

Peabody Picture Vocabulary Test—Revised

Standard Score: 105
Percentile: 63
Age Equivalent: 9 years, 4 months
Stanine: 6

Developmental Test of Visual Motor Integration—Revised

Age Equivalent: 8 years, 9 months
Standard Score: 102
Percentile: 55

Woodcock-Johnson Psychoeducational Battery—Revised
Tests of Achievement

	Age Score	Grade Score	Standard Score	%ile
Letter-Word Identification	7.8	2.1	89	24
Passage Comprehension	9.2	3.6	109	72
Word Attack	7.10	2.2	94	36
Calculation	8.3	2.8	96	40
Applied Problems	9.11	4.4	119	90
Quantitative Concepts	8.5	3.0	98	46
Dictation	7.8	2.2	91	27
Writing Samples	8.1	2.8	98	44
Science	10.8	5.2	121	92
Social Studies	9.1	3.7	107	68
Humanities	10.8	5.3	117	87
Broad Reading			96	40
Broad Mathematics			109	72
Broad Written Language			92	31
Broad Knowledge			115	84
Skills			95	37

Kagan Matching Familiar Figures Test: Below average

Woodcock-Johnson Tests of Cognitive Ability

	Age Score	Grade Score
Numbers Reversed	8.8	3.4
Memory for Sentences	4.8	K.0
Memory for Words	7.7	2.3

Interpretation of Test Results

The results of today's educational evaluation fall generally in the average to low average range, except for the areas of sight word identification, spelling, and writing samples. This pattern suggests relatively greater difficulty with sight word identification, which is consistent with results of previous testing of mental processing by Dr. X. MB demonstrates significant ability in mathematics, particularly in the area of mathematics applications. However, she had difficulty with calculations due to poor recall for facts and impulsivity. At times when doing the problems, MB subtracted without looking at the operator, which was an addition sign, and she hurried through the section. The general knowledge section of the *Woodcock-Johnson* demonstrates good information and vocabulary skills, and places MB's ability at the fifth-grade level. Difficulties in memory and recall for short-term information were demonstrated throughout the testing. When we compare MB's present standard scores to the psychometric summary on the *Wechsler*, we see a significant discrepancy in ability versus achievement.

Complete results reflect significant variability in MB's performance on different types of tasks, ranging from superior skills in application of mathematics to average reasoning skills to significantly below average memory performance in spelling and letter-word identification. Such a profile is consistent with the teacher's observations and Mr. and Mrs. B.'s comments regarding MB's difficulties with listening and saying things that have little or no connection to what is going on. Based on MB's performance on the full-scale IQ test, she would be expected to attain above average scores on achievement tests. Her performance today on the *Woodcock-Johnson* indicates that MB's actual achievement levels in reading, math, and written language are all average or below average, consistently below predicted levels. Throughout testing, MB's degree of attention to task varied widely, and her poor performance on some subtests (for example, Memory for Sentences) could be attributed to these attention lapses.

On the *Developmental Test of Visual Motor Integration*, MB's performance resulted in a standard score of 102, which is equivalent to the 55th percentile.

On the *ANSER School Questionnaire*, MB's teacher rated MB's behavior as below normal limits compared to other girls her age and reported significant difficulties in listening, impulsivity, and inattention.

Summary and Recommendations

MB is a bright young lady who exhibits a wide range of behaviors in various settings. In school, her teacher relates that she has difficulty attending to task and completing written language and reading activities. At home, her parents observe that an inordinate amount of effort is required for MB to succeed in school tasks. In the context of individual testing conducted by two different examiners on different occasions, MB's behavior is characterized by distractibility, impulsivity, and difficulty with memory tasks. The teacher reports that at times MB can be a daydreamer. This was observed during individual testing today, as well.

When reviewing current educational testing compared with testing from 1989, there appear to be significant variability and discrepancies. Current testing suggests that MB's behavior is consistent with the previous diagnosis of an attention deficit disorder, a condition associated with mild chronic neuropsychological dysfunction. Most of the time in the classroom, this condition occurs with some hyperactivity. MB is reported as having difficulty following directions and initiating work on a task. When she works independently, MB may exhibit signs such as fidgeting and impulsivity, as were observed today during individual testing.

In addition to signs of an attention deficit disorder, current testing suggests some other weakness in higher-order cognitive skills. Hence, despite MB's superior verbal skills, she has some difficulty in planning, organization, and recall of sequential information. I believe some of these difficulties are causing frustration for MB, and she is not performing to her highest level of ability. MB's problems are subtle yet quite real and are consistent with her parents' and teacher's observations of difficulties.

MB would respond to help from a tutor in going over material and continually reinforcing strategies for attention and concentration. MB would also benefit from some tutoring in academic areas. The academic curriculum at St. Luke Parochial School is challenging, and MB will need continual reinforcement to feel successful in her current class placement. She may be eligible for some special programming in a public school, although services of this sort are not offered at St. Luke. Her parents will want to take this report to their local public school and ask whether further testing could be conducted to determine whether MB is eligible to receive some support within her home school environment.

The following approaches might be explored:

1. In addition to some tutoring or perhaps special services through the public school, MB will need to develop some strategies that use her visual strengths in the area of spelling. She has difficulty with attention to detail in spelling and with remembering items such as grammar, capitalization, and punctuation. To improve her writing and spelling, MB's parents may want to promote the following study program at home.

   a. After receiving spelling words at school, MB should decide which words she knows and which ones she needs to study. Then, typing the words on a computer or typewriter or using magnetic letters to spell out the words will provide a multisensory approach that supports attention to detail.

   b. On the second night, MB can spell the words into a tape recorder and play them back.

   c. On the third night, MB can write the words on a variety of different media—such as with large felt markers on paper, on a chalkboard with chalk, or with a finger in talcum powder—to increase visual imprinting of spelling patterns.

   In addition, as MB matures, she may enjoy using a hand speller on her desk in the classroom or at home. This will assist her in the visual imprinting of spelling patterns as she uses them daily in her work. The use of a word processor or computer spelling package will also be helpful as she gets older.

2. Whenever possible, MB should be seated near the teacher and away from distractors such as windows, interesting centers in the room, and talkative classmates. An area where she can move around will be helpful for her.

3. MB performs better in a small, highly routine classroom environment (like that at St. Luke) that is characterized by frequent opportunities for organization and rehearsal.

4. Consistent cooperation between home and school is highly advisable.

5. MB's academic skills should be assessed individually at the end of the third grade to ensure that she is making adequate progress in the classroom. Should she show undue frustration in school prior to that time, a team meeting should be scheduled immediately.

6. Systematic instruction in abstract reasoning and concept formation, beginning with such elements as observing similarities, categorization, and color-coding particular letters and words for recall will be helpful.

7. Mnemonics—the use of tricks, patterns, and unusual formations of letters may be helpful to increase MB's memory for facts. *Facts on Tape* is available through a teacher's supply outlet. There are subtraction, multiplication, and addition tapes which may be very supportive to MB as she attempts to learn these facts for quick recall.

Chapter 9
Resources

National Newsletters

Challenge, a newsletter on Attention-Deficit/Hyperactivity Disorder
P.O. Box 2001
West Newbury, MA 01985
(508) 462-0495

CHADDER, a bi-annual publication of CH.A.D.D.
499 N.W. 70th Avenue, Suite 308
Plantation, FL 33317
(305) 587-3700
Fax: (305) 587-4599

Advance, a publication of ADDAG
8091 S. Ireland Way
Aurora, CO 80016
(303) 690-7548

Attention Please, a newsletter for children with Attention Deficit Disorder
2106 3rd Avenue, N.
Seattle, WA 98109-2305

Kids Getting You Down?
Learning Development Services
3754 Clairemont Drive
San Diego, CA 92117

National Organizations

A.D.D.A. Attention Deficit Disorder Association
8091 South Ireland Way
Aurora, CO 80016
(303) 690-7548

American Academy of Child and Adolescent Psychiatry
3615 Wisconsin Avenue, N.W.
Washington, DC 20016
(202) 966-7300

American Academy of Family Physicians
8880 Ward Parkway
Kansas City, MO 64114--2797

American Academy of Pediatrics
P.O. Box 927
Elk Grove Village, IL 60009
(312) 981-7935

American Family Therapy Association
2550 M Street, N.E., Suite 275
Washington, DC 20037

American Psychological Association
1200 17th Street, N.W.
Washington, DC 20036
(202) 955-7618

American School Counselors Association
5999 Stevenson Avenue
Alexandria, VA 22304
(703) 823-9800

American School Help Association
P.O. Box 708
Kent, OH 44240

Association of Educational Therapists
P.O. Box 946
Woodland Hills, CA 91365
(818) 788-3850

Council for Exceptional Children
1920 Association Drive
Reston, VA 22091
(703) 620-3660

Children and Adults with Attention Deficit Disorders (CH.A.D.D.)
499 N.W. 70th Avenue, Suite 308
Plantation, FL 33317
(305) 587-3700

There are local CH.A.D.D. support groups in every state, plus some foreign countries. Local groups meet once or twice a month, and are open to both members and nonmembers of CH.A.D.D. Call the National Office for information on contacting a group in your area.

Foundation for Children with Learning Disabilities
99 Park Avenue
New York, NY 10016
(212) 687-7211

Learning Disabilities Association
4156 Library Road
Pittsburgh, PA 15234
(412) 341-1515

National Information Center for Handicapped Children and Youth
P.O. Box 1492
Washington, DC 20013
(703) 893-6061

202

Videotapes

Why Won't My Child Pay Attention?, by Sam Goldstein, Ph.D.

It's Just Attention Disorder, A Video for Kids, by Sam Goldstein, Ph.D., and Michael Goldstein, M.D.

Both are available from:
Neurology Learning and Behavior Center
230 S. 500 E., Suite 100
Salt Lake City, UT 84102

ADHD, What Do We Know?, by Russell Barkley, Ph.D.

ADHD, What Can We Do?, by Russell Barkley, Ph.D.

Both are available from:
Guilford Publications
72 Spring Street
New York, NY 10012
(800) 365-7006

ADHD in Adulthood, A Clinical Perspective, by Arthur Robin, Ph.D.
Available from
ADD Warehouse
300 N.W. 70th Avenue, Suite 102
Plantation, FL 33317
(800) 233-9273

Suggested Reading Materials

ADD Hyperactivity Workbook, by Harvey C. Parker, Ph.D.
Impact Publications
Available from ADD Warehouse
300 N.W. 70th Avenue, Suite 102
Plantation, FL 33317

All Kinds of Minds,
Developmental Variation in Learning Disorders, and
Keeping Ahead in School, by Mel Levine, Ph.D.
Educators Publishing Services, Inc.
75 Moulton Street
Cambridge, MA 02138-1104

Attention Deficit Disorder and Hyperactivity, and
Attention Deficit Hyperactivity Disorder, by Russell Barkley, Ph.D.
PRO-ED
8700 Shoal Creek Blvd.
Austin, TX 78757-6897

The Hyperactive Child, Adolescent and Adult, by Paul H. Wender
Oxford University Press
200 Madison Ave.
New York, NY 10016

I Can't Sit Still: Educating and Affirming Inattentive and Hyperactive Children, by Dorothy Davies Johnson, M.D.
ETR Associates
P.O. Box 1830
Santa Cruz, CA 95061-1830

Managing Attention Disorders in Children, by Sam Goldstein, Ph.D., and Michael Goldstein, M.D.
John Wiley and Sons
605 3rd Ave.
New York, NY 10158-00012

Maybe You Know My Kid: A Parent's Guide to Identifying, Understanding and Helping Your Child with Attention Deficit Hyperactivity Disorder, by Mary Cahill Fowler
Birch Lane Press
600 Madison Ave.
New York, NY 10022

Sourcebook for Children with Attention Deficit Disorder: A Management Guide for Early Childhood Professionals and Parents, by Clare B. Jones, Ph.D.
Communication Skill Builders
P.O. Box 42050
Tucson, AZ 85733

Teaching Students Ways to Remember: Strategies for Learning Mnemonically, by Margo A. Mastropieri and Thomas E. Scruggs
Teaching Test-Taking Skills: Helping Students Show What They Know, by Thomas E. Scruggs and Margo A. Mastropieri
Brookline Books
P.O. Box 1046
Cambridge, MA 02238-1046

Toward Positive Classroom Discipline, by Harvey F. Clarizio
John Wiley and Sons
605 3rd Ave.
New York, NY 10158-0012

Why Johnny Can't Concentrate: Coping with Attention Deficit Problems, by Robert A. Moss, M.D., with Helen Huff Funlat
Bantam Doubleday Dell Publishing
1540 Broadway
New York, NY 10036

Your Hyperactive Child: A Parent's Guide to Coping with Attention Deficit Disorder, by Barbara D. Ingersoll, Ph.D.
Bantam Doubleday Dell Publishing
1540 Broadway
New York, NY 10036

Attention Deficit Disorder and Learning Disabilities: Realities, Myths, and Controversial Treatments, by Barbara D. Ingersoll, Ph.D., and Sam Goldstein, Ph.D.
Bantam Doubleday Dell Publishing
1540 Broadway
New York, NY 10036

Attention Deficit Disorder in Adults, by Lynn Weiss, Ph.D.
Taylor Publishing
Trade Books Division
1550 West Mockingbird Lane
Dallas, TX 75235
800-759-8120

What Is Attention Deficit Disorder (ADD or ADHD)?

Attention deficit disorder is a term used to describe children who are inattentive, impulsive, and frequently also very active at levels that are higher than expected for their mental and chronological age.

Who Can Diagnose ADD (ADHD)?

Children with attention deficits benefit from an evaluation by a multidisciplinary team. The team might be based in a medical, educational, mental health, or other facility. Effective interdisciplinary collaboration is essential in order to identify all the child's needs.

What Are the Diagnostic Criteria for ADD (ADHD)?

The presence of any eight of the following 15 symptoms over a minimum of six months is necessary for the diagnosis to be made. These symptoms should be present prior to age seven (that is, during the preschool years) to ensure that these behaviors are not merely a reaction to school.

DSM IV Draft Criteria for Attention-Deficit/Hyperactivity Disorder

A. Either (1) or (2):

(1) Inattention: At least six of the following symptoms of inattention have persisted for at least six months to a degree that is maladaptive and inconsistent with developmental level:

(a) often fails to give close attention to details or makes careless mistakes in schoolwork, work, or other activities.

(b) often has difficulty sustaining attention in tasks or play activities

(c) often does not seem to listen to what is being said to him or her

(d) often does not follow through on instructions and fails to finish schoolwork, chores, or duties in the workplace (not due to oppositional behavior or failure to understand instructions)

(e) often has difficulties organizing tasks and activities

(f) often avoids or strongly dislikes tasks (such as schoolwork or homework) that require sustained mental effort

(g) often loses things necessary for tasks or activities (e.g., school assignments, pencils, books, tools, or toys)

(h) is often easily distracted by extraneous stimuli

(i) often forgetful in daily activities

(2) Hyperactivity-Impulsivity: At least four of the following symptoms of hyperactivity-impulsivity have persisted for at least six months to a degree that is maladaptive and inconsistent with developmental level:

Hyperactivity

(a) often fidgets with hands or feet or squirms in seat

(b) leaves seat in classroom or in other situations in which remaining seated is expected

(c) often runs about or climbs excessively in situations where it is inappropriate (in adolescents or adults, may be limited to subjective feelings of restlessness)

(d) often has difficulty playing or engaging in leisure activities quietly

Impulsivity

(e) often blurts out answers to questions before the questions have been completed

(f) often has difficulty waiting in lines or awaiting turn in games or group situations

B. Onset no later than seven years of age.

C. Symptoms must be present in two or more situations (e.g., at school, work, and at home).

D. The disturbance causes clinically significant distress or impairment in social, academic, or occupational functioning.

E. Does not occur exclusively during the course of a Pervasive Developmental Disorder, Schizophrenia or other Psychotic Disorder, and is not better accounted for by a Mood Disorder, Anxiety Disorder, Dissociative Disorder, or a Personality Disorder.

What Are the Possible Causes of ADD (ADHD)?

Researchers stress that no conclusive evidence exists for a single cause of ADD, but multiple genetic, prenatal, and physical cofactors need to be considered. The rate at which the brain uses glucose also appears to be lower in subjects with ADD.

What Are Educational Accommodations?

The child is generally placed in a regular classroom under the management of the classroom teacher, possibly with additional support services, if the child qualifies for special education.

Intervention techniques teachers can employ that help students succeed in the classroom include the following: preferential seating; activities which offer brevity, variety, and structure; avoidance of unnecessary detail; less intense detail; and smaller chunks of required work. Students need strategies to help them finish their work, slow down and control their movements, and remember information.

What Are Some Medical Options?

All youngsters with ADD should be referred to a physician for a physical examination. Many children benefit from psychostimulant medication, counseling, and behavior modification.

Note: The draft diagnostic criteria for attention deficit disorder are reproduced with permission from the forthcoming *Diagnostic and statistical manual of mental disorders.* 4th ed. Washington, DC: American Psychiatric Association, 1994.

References

Abramowitz, A., and S. O'Leary. 1991. Behavioral interventions for the classroom: Implications for students with ADHD. *School Psychology Review* 20(2):220-34.

Achenbach, T. M., and C. S. Edelbrock. 1983. Child behavior checklist and revised child behavior profile. Burlington, VT: Department of Psychiatry, University of Vermont.

Adams, A., and Alinder, M. S. 1990. *Ansel Adams: A biography.* Boston, MA: Bullfinch Press.

American Psychiatric Association. in press. *Diagnostic and statistical manual of mental disorders.* 4th ed. Washington, DC: American Psychiatric Association.

Armstrong, T. 1987. *In their own way.* New York: Jeremy P. Tarcher.

Barkley, R. A. 1981. *Hyperactive children: A handbook for diagnosis and treatment.* New York: Guilford Press.

_____. 1990. *Attention deficit hyperactivity disorder: A handbook for diagnosis and treatment.* New York: Guilford Press.

Bauwens, J., and J. Hourcode. 1989. Hey, would you just listen? *Teaching Exceptional Children* 21 (Summer): 22-61.

Bee, H. 1979. *The developing child.* New York: Harper and Row.

Beery, K., and N. A. Buktenica. 1967. *The developmental test of visual motor integration (Beery VMI)—Revised.* Cleveland, OH: Modern Curriculum Press.

Braswell, L., and M. Bloomquist. 1991. *Attention deficits and hyperactivity: A model for child, family and school intervention.* New York: Guilford Press.

Brophy, J., and T. Good. 1974. *Teacher-student relationships—Causes and consequences.* New York: Holt, Rinehart, and Winston.

Bulgren, J. A., J. B. Schumaker, and D. Deshler. 1988. Effectiveness of a concept teaching routine in enhancing the performance of LD students in secondary-level mainstream classes. *Learning Disability Quarterly* 11(1): 3-17.

_____. 1993. *The concept mastery routine.* Lawrence, KS: Edge Enterprises, Inc.

Cantwell, D. P. 1979. The hyperactive child. *Hospital Practice* 14: 650-73.

Carman, R. A., and W. R. Adams. 1972. *Study skills: A student's guide for survival.* New York: John Wiley and Sons.

Carmine, D. 1990. Cognatic research on design principles. *Research and Resources on Special Education Abstract* 27.

Charles, C. M. 1989. *Building classroom discipline: From models to practice.* New York and London: Longman.

Clarizio, H. 1976. *Toward positive classroom discipline.* New York: John Wiley and Sons.

Comings, D. E. 1990. *Tourette's syndrome and human behavior.* Duarte: Hope Press.

Conners, K. 1980. *Food additives and hyperactive children.* New York: Plenum Press.

———. 1989. *Conners' teacher and parent rating scales.* Toronto: Multi-Health Systems.

Cooke, J., and D. Williams. 1987. *Working with Children's Language.* Tucson, AZ: Communication Skill Builders.

Council for Exceptional Children. March, 1990. Student self management to increase on-task behaviors. CEC Research Brief T3. Reston, VA: Council for Exceptional Children.

Douglas, V. I. 1983. Attention and cognitive problems. In *Developmental neuropsychiatry,* edited by N. M. Rudder, 280-329. New York: Guilford Press.

Douglas, V. I., and K. G. Peters. 1979. Toward a clear definition of attentional deficits of hyperactive children. In *Attention and cognitive development,* edited by N. E. A. Hale, and M. Lewis, 173-247. New York: Plenum Press.

Dreikurs, R. B. Grunwald, and F. Pepper. 1971. *Maintaining sanity in the classroom.* New York: Harper and Row.

DuPaul, G. J., M. Rapport, and L. M. Perriello. 1990. Teacher ratings of academic performance: The development of the academic performance rating scale. Worcester, MA: Department of Psychiatry, Worcester State University.

Edelbrock, C. 1988. Child attention problems checklist (CAP). Worcester, MA: Department of Psychiatry, Worcester State University.

Friedman, R., and G. Doyal. 1992. *Management of children and adolescents with attention deficit hyperactivity disorder.* Austin, TX: PRO-ED.

Gardner, H. 1987. Multiple learning styles. In *In their own way,* by T. Armstrong, 10-28. New York: Jeremy P. Tarcher.

Goldstein, S., and M. Goldstein. 1990. *Managing attention disorders in children.* New York: John Wiley and Sons.

Goldstein, S., and M. Pollock. 1988. *Teacher observation checklist.* Salt Lake City: Neurology, Learning, and Behavior Center.

Hammill, D. D. 1985. *Detroit tests of learning aptitude.* 2d ed. Austin, TX: PRO-ED.

Hartsough, C. S., and N. M. Lambert. 1985. Medical factors in hyperactive and normal children. *American Journal of Orthopsychiatry* 55:190-201.

Hauser, P. 1993. ADHD in people with generalized resistance to thyroid hormone. *New England Journal of Medicine* 329 (14):997-1001.

Hepworth, J., C. B. Jones, and C. Sehested. 1991. Teacher survey of ADHD in Arizona third and fourth grade children. College of Nursing, Arizona State University. Unpublished research study.

Ingersoll, B. D., and S. Goldstein. 1993. *Attention deficit disorder and learning disabilities: Realities, myths, and controversial treatments.* New York: Doubleday.

Johnson, D. D. 1992. *I can't sit still: Educating and affirming inattentive and hyperactive children.* Santa Cruz, CA: ETR Associates.

Jones, C. B. 1986. Bridging the generation gap: Techniques. *Journal for Remedial Education and Counseling* 2:182.

_____. 1989. Managing the difficult child. *Family Day Caring* (Nov/Dec): 6-7.

_____. 1991. *Sourcebook for children with attention deficit disorder: A management guide for early childhood professionals and parents.* Tucson, AZ: Communication Skill Builders.

_____. 1993. The young and the restless. *CHADDER Newsletter.* September.

Jones, F. 1987. *Positive classroom discipline.* New York: McGraw-Hill.

Jones, V. F., and L. S. Jones. 1986. *Comprehensive classroom management: Creating positive learning environments.* Boston: Allyn and Bacon.

Klee, S., B. Garfinkel, and H. Beauchesne. 1986. Attention deficits in adults. *Psychiatric Annals* 16 (Jan.):1.

Koskovich, K. 1992. Fun games and learning with Karen Koskovich. *Strategram* 4(4):7-81.

Kuker, R., B. Drumwall, and F. Pepper. 1971. *Maintaining sanity in the classroom.* New York: Harper and Row.

Lakein, A. 1973. *How to get control of your time and your life.* New York: New American Library.

Lambert, N. M., J. Sandoval, and D. Sassone. 1978. Prevalence of hyperactivity in elementary school children as a function of social system definers. *American Journal of Orthopsychiatry* 48:446-63.

Levine, M. 1985. *The ANSER System.* Cambridge, MA: Educators Publishing Service.

_____. 1987a. *Developmental variation and learning disorders.* Cambridge, MA: Educators Publishing Service.

_____. 1987b. Attention disorders: The diverse effects of weak control systems in childhood. *Pediatric Annals* 16(2):117-30.

Liberman, L. 1986. *Special educator's guide.* Weston, MA: Nobb Hill Press.

Loney, J., J. Kramer, and R. Milich. 1981. The hyperkinetic child grows up: Predictors of symptoms, delinquency and achievement at follow-up. In *Psychosocial aspects of drug treatment for hyperactivity,* edited by K. D. Gadow and J. Loney. Boulder, CO: Westview Press.

Lovitt, T. C., and J. O. Smith. 1972. Effects of instructions on an individual's verbal behavior. *Teaching Exceptional Children* 38:685-93.

Lund, K. A., and C. S. Bos. 1981. Orchestrating the preschool classroom: The daily schedule. *Teaching Exceptional Children* 14:120-25.

McCarney, S. B. 1989. *Attention deficit disorders intervention manual.* Columbia, MO: Hawthorne Educational Services.

Margolies, B. 1990. Attention deficit and the Macintosh. *Macintosh Lab Monitor* 9:11-13.

Mashburn, S. 1991. Strategies for the ADD adolescent. Unpublished classroom assignment.

Mastropieri, M. A. 1988. Using the keyword method. *Teaching Exceptional Children,* 20:4-8.

Mastropieri, M. A., and T. Scruggs. 1991. *Teaching students ways to remember: Strategies for learning mnemonically.* Cambridge, MA: Brookline Books.

Milich, R. S., and J. Loney. 1979. The role of hyperactive and aggressive symptomatology in predicting adolescent outcome among hyperactive children. *Journal of Pediatric Psychology* 4:93-112.

Mirsky, A. F. 1978. Attention: A neuropsychological perspective. In *Education and the brain,* edited by J. S. Shall, and A. F. Mirsky, 33-60. Chicago: National Society for the Study of Education.

Mueser, A. 1981. *Reading aids through the grades.* New York: Teachers College.

Murphy, J. 1989. *Toughing out Tourette's and attention deficit.* Baton Rouge, LA: Tourette's Syndrome Support Group.

Murphy, K. 1992. Coping strategies for ADHD adults. *CHADDER* 6(2):10-11.

Prelutsky, J. 1984. *The new kid on the block.* New York: Greenwillow Books.

Robinson, F. P. 1969. SQ3R method of reading. In *SR/SE resource book,* edited by F. L. Christ, 35-40. New York: Harper.

Rosenshine, B. V. 1980. How time is spent in elementary classrooms. In *Time to learn,* edited by C. Denham and A. Lieberman. 107-26. Washington, DC: National Institute of Education.

Salend, S. J. 1990. *Effective mainstreaming.* New York: Macmillan.

Scheiber, B. and J. Talpers. 1987. *Unlocking potential: College and other choices for learning disabled people.* Bethesda, MD: Adler and Adler.

Schlegel, M., and C. Bos. 1986. STORE the story: Fiction/fantasy reading comprehension and writing strategy. Department of Special Education and Rehabilitation, Tucson, AZ. Photocopy.

Schrag, J. 1992. ADD eligibility. *Education of the Handicapped* 18(11):5.

Schumaker, J. B., D. D. Deshler, G. R. Alley, M. M. Warner, F. Clark, and S. Nolan. 1982. Error monitoring: A learning strategy for improving adolescent performance. In *Best of ACLD,* vol. 3, edited by W. M. Cruekshank and J. Lerner, 170-82. Syracuse, NY: Syracuse University Press.

Scruggs, T., and M. Mastropieri. 1992. *Teaching test taking skills: Helping students show what they know.* Cambridge, MA: Brookline Books.

Shaywitz, B. A. 1987. *Yale children's inventory.* New Haven, CT: Yale University Medical School.

Shaywitz, S. E., and B. A. Shaywitz. 1991. Attention deficit disorder: Current perspectives. In *Learning disabilities: Proceedings of the national conference, 1988,* edited by J. F. Kavanough and T. J. Truss, 369-523. Parkton, MD: York Press.

Silver, L. B. 1989. Learning disabilities. *Journal of the American Academy of Child and Adolescent Psychiatry* 20:309-13.

Smith, C. B., and P. Elliott. 1979. *Reading activities for middle and secondary schools: A handbook for teachers.* New York: Holt, Rinehart and Winston.

Swanson, J. 1993. Update on the multi-modal treatments of ADD. Paper presented to the CH.A.D.D. Conference, Professional Institute. Audiocassette #93-1523.

Telzrow, C. F., and B. Speer. 1986. Learning disabled children: General instructions for maximizing instruction. *Techniques: A Journal for Remedial Education and Counseling* 2:341-52.

Tonjes, M. J., and M. V. Zintz. 1981. *Teaching reading/thinking/study skills in content classrooms.* Dubuque, IA: William C. Brown.

Ullmann, R. K., E. K. Sleator, and R. K. Sprague. 1985. *ADD-H comprehensive teacher's rating scale (ACTeRS)*. Champaign, IL: MeriTech.

Wechsler, D. 1974. *Wechsler intelligence scale for children III*. San Antonio, TX: The Psychological Corporation.

Weiss, G., and L. T. Hechtman. 1986. *Hyperactive children grown up*. New York: Guilford Press.

Wender, P. 1971. *Minimal brain dysfunction in children*. New York: Wiley-Interscience.

_____. 1987. *The hyperactive child, adolescent and adult: Attention deficit disorder through the life span*. New York: Oxford University Press.

Woodcock, R. W., and M. B. Johnson. 1989. *Woodcock-Johnson psychoeducational and cognitive batteries—Revised*. Allen, TX: DLM Teaching Resources.

Wyngaarden, J. B. 1988. Adverse effects of low-level lead exposure on infant development. *Journal of the American Medical Association* 259:2524.

Yudofsky, S., R. Hales, and T. Ferguson. 1991. *What you need to know about psychiatric drugs*. New York: Ballantine Books.

Zametkin, A., T. Nordahl, M. Cross, D. King, W. Semple, J. Rumsey, S. Hamburger, and R. Cohen. 1990. Cerebral glucose metabolism in adults with hyperactivity of childhood onset. *The New England Journal of Medicine* 323(20):1361-66.

Zentall, S. S. 1986. Effects of color stimulation on performance and activity of hyperactive and non-hyperactive children. *Journal of Educational Psychology* 78:159-65.

Zentall, S. S., and T. Kruczek. 1988. The attraction of colors for active attention problem children. *Exceptional Children* 54(4):357-62.